MW00337768

The In Between

Copyright © 2020 Jim Bruton

## THE IN BETWEEN

All rights reserved. No part of this publication may be reproduced, distributed, or transmitted in any form or by any means, including photocopying, recording, or other electronic or mechanical methods, without the prior written permission of the publisher, except in the case of brief quotations embodied in critical reviews and certain other noncommercial uses permitted by copyright law. For permission requests, write to the publisher, addressed "Attention: Permissions Coordinator," at info@beyondpublishing.net

Quantity sales special discounts are available on quantity purchases by corporations, associations, and others. For details, contact the publisher at the address above.

Orders by U.S. trade bookstores and wholesalers. Email info@BeyondPublishing. net

The Beyond Publishing Speakers Bureau can bring authors to your live event. For more information or to book an event contact the Beyond Publishing Speakers Bureau speak@BeyondPublishing.net

The Author can be reached directly at BeyondPublishing.net

Manufactured and printed in the United States of America distributed globally by BeyondPublishing.net

New York | Los Angeles | London | Sydney

ISBN Hardcover: 978-1-952884-73-3

ISBN Softcover: 978-1-952884-97-9

# The
# In Between

## A Trip of a Lifetime

Jim Bruton

# Contents

"An insightful memoir from a man who actually fell from the skies. Jim Bruton discovers a "rebirth" of his true-life purpose and direction after experiencing an NDE while recovering from serious injuries from an airplane crash. Coming to grips with who he was, who he is, and will be, creates a stream of consciousness that questions even his own reality and forever alters his life choices. A must-read story for true spiritual seekers that needs to be shared. Fasten your seat belt as you begin to read Jim's life story."

> Reverend Bill McDonald, author of *Warrior:*
> *A Spiritual Odyssey* and *Alchemy of Warrior's Heart*

"Jim Bruton has lived a life few can imagine. For a man with his remarkable experiences, it took a near fatal crash of the airplane he built, and his near-death experience, to convince him to tell his story. The In Between is a riveting and spiritual memoir, guaranteed to make readers examine their own lives and purpose."

> Tilghman G. Pitts III, former chairman of
> Oppenheimer Funds Distributors

Jim Bruton's dramatic story shows clearly how an NDE can differ from the familiar pattern of "light and love" yet alter a life completely. His experience is more cognitive than emotional, yet in dealing with its effects, he must reckon with the challenges familiar to all experiencers—a new sense of reality, synchronicities, altered vision, and public disbelief. An excellent introduction to a variant type of near-death experience.

> Nancy Evans Bush, author of *Dancing Past the*
> *Dark: Distressing Near Death Experiences*

## Dedication

To those who have sometimes used a carrot but more often used a stick to get me this far. I'm sure we will arrive at a place one day that we can laugh about it. Until then, thank you for your patience- I hope the wait will have been worth it.

Part I:

# The Synchronicity that Changed Everything

Chapter One:

# The Light Bulb Turns On

The sun was setting and if I was going to catch the green flash, it would be soon and come quickly. If I blinked my eyes at the wrong instant, I would miss it. Years of practice staring at the world through a film camera's viewfinder gave me the patience for this task. Unexpectedly, three hundred miles from almost anyone else, I heard the low hum of a car engine. Then several. I allowed myself the momentary distraction of looking with my other eye at the undulating horizon of sand dunes within my limited range of vision, not taking my working eye away from the viewfinder. As the possible moment approached that the sun's angle, the earth's atmospheric refraction and everything else between my eye and the sun might align perfectly to flash for a moment one of the rarest things seen, a flash of green light before the sun dropped below the horizon, I found the increasing volume of the 4-wheel drive vehicles distracting and annoying. A minute more and I realized that today wasn't the day the green flash would appear. However, the caravan of vehicles did, topping the dune's ridge and driving toward me. Frustration forgotten, I watched with interest while the lead vehicle, driven by one of the park ranger's I knew, pulled up near me. Those following came to a stop and I walked up to the ranger to ask what brought him to right where I was. His party in tow was a Disney film crew, scouting locations for a future movie. As he and I talked, I saw the team pull some cases out of the back of one car and open a flexible satellite dish. My eyebrows raised in curiosity and I walked over to them. They plugged in a series of cables to a large metal box, including a telephone handset. I asked what this device was and they told me it was a satellite telephone. Then they punched in a long set of numbers on the phone's handset and I considered how remotely situated I was, in the middle of nowhere in a country called Namibia, which itself means "The Big Nothing". And here I was, in that big nothing, watching people use a telephone that could talk to anyone, anywhere, instantly. I loved the small satellite dish- it looked like something from a science fiction movie, positioned atop the sand dune. I asked one of the crew if anyone had ever pushed video over such a system. They didn't know. This was in 1993 and with the recent advent of the World Wide Web to give some order to the internet, right then and there I considered the possibility to be able to go live with video from similarly remote places into the internet. I could see so many uses of such a capability, from augmenting my wildlife film work with a "Live from the Waterhole" component, to how live news feeds could change, to connecting school children around the world and building a sense of community beyond what we knew then. In that moment, I knew I was going to solve this problem.

My name is Jim Bruton and this is my story.

***

How did I get to the top of that sand dune, where my destiny was waiting for me?

It began with the planting of a seed. When I was a little boy, like many others growing up in the 1960s, I loved reading *Popular Mechanics*, wondering when we would get the promised rocket pack that I could fly to school, or what tourism to the moon would be like in the far off and idealized year of 2000. I also loved old airplanes because of the adventure and continual discovery they represented. But every Sunday night, I sat down to watch on our small black and white television the *Wonderful World of Disney* and then *Wild Kingdom*. Disney fueled my imagination and dreams like *Popular Mechanics'* visions of the future. *Wild Kingdom* increased my love for animals and travel to exotic, far-off places.

One night, as I sat there watching Jim Fowler climb a tree before an angry animal caught him, I asked, "How do I do that for a living?" As a mentor would one day tell me, "That was as good as a prayer."

Between putting my cosmic order in and waiting for it to finish cooking, I had a lot of growing up to do. Even though a non-typical person, I had an average childhood which included moving to another state, making new friends, school athletics and so on. I discovered surprise aptitudes such as martial arts, bicycle racing and tennis while realizing I had no talent for football, baseball or basketball. So I focused on what I was good at and occasionally thought of my childhood dreams of travel and adventure.

At some point in university, I met Julie Bartlett through a mutual friend in Charlotte, NC whose father and mother, Des and Jen, made wildlife films and their experience went back to almost the birth of wildlife film-making. As a young man, Des worked for Armand Denis, who was active in the business in the 1950s and 1960s. Des met Jen on a trip back to his native Australia, and she was playing tennis at venues like Wimbledon. Somehow, he talked her into giving up all that and returning to Africa with him. Julie was born soon thereafter and grew up in an Africa we haven't seen for a long time.

One of her photos I first saw was holding hands with pygmies in the Congo- she was dressed in a perfect little dress and the locals were dressed in their more...minimal fashion. She was the subject of the book *Growing Up With Animals* and helped raise some amazing creatures which were also her only playmates. Some of her schooling was at home but then she was shipped off to a Victorian-style boarding school in Australia with a tradition of hats and gloves on Sundays. She graduated from high school and decided to pursue a degree in marine biology.

After consulting with some world-class experts (like Sylvia Earle), she settled on Queens College (now Queens University) in Charlotte. It would be a few more years, after we both graduated in fact, but through a mutual friend we met and after dating for a while, I mentioned what her father did as one of my childhood dreams, asked if he ever needed any help, she asked, he said yes and that was the first step to that providential meeting with Disney on the sand dune.

The first two years I lived in Namibia were difficult in some ways, but more in terms of my adjustment than for any other reason. I was twenty-three years old and very much a product of my culture. I was used to a high degree of stimulation and moving to a game park in Africa was like hitting the brakes from a high-speed car. With no radio, no television, no internet and not a large social circle or activities to choose from, it was a challenging adjustment.

Filming wildlife takes great patience and a comfort with uncertainty- you can't script things, like when the lion hiding next to a game trail or in the tall grass near a water hole will suddenly pounce on an unsuspecting gazelle. Filming the hatching of an ostrich egg? Try sitting there from first to last light of the day, several days in a row, with your eye glued to the camera. And finding the same zebra in a herd of a thousand every day and following her around, hoping to catch her giving birth, only to arrive one day and see that she had her foal in the night. That takes a special mindset.

Most days, when possible, I read a lot of novels. Sometimes I made things, like a bow and arrows, using the same techniques the locals used. I shot footage and took a lot of still photos too. But it was a major shift to settle down into a different pace of life with different things to keep me focused.

The second year was easier- I felt like the first year was tearing down and the next year was re-building up from there. But I was becoming restless and had some crazy thought from the little correspondence I received from a few friends back in the USA that life was exciting and ever-changing for them while it was pretty static for me. At the end of my second year away, Julie and I returned home to Charlotte.

While figuring life out from that perspective, we started a silkscreen business for printing bottles- shampoo, pharmaceuticals, hair products, chemicals, etc. One of Julie's friends ran a halfway house for unwed mothers two blocks away from our business, so that seemed a synergy of mutual benefit with the bonus of feeling good about helping the down and out. During this idealistic time of trying to save the world, I figured out how to silkscreen a bar code and the Department of Defense who invented bar codes, called me and said I was the first person in the world they knew of who could do it, silk-screening to an accuracy of $1/5000^{th}$ of an inch. I never did save the world with employed unwed mothers but I hope I helped a little. I did use my high-quality printing processes to get more business. I even came up with a conductive ink that could be silkscreened onto fabric and connected to a cattle prod to prevent someone from simply grabbing you or to create mats that cats would avoid when wanting to leave footprints on your freshly washed car.

Eventually I lost interest in this huge time/low profit business model and Julie and I started Old World Safaris. We felt there wasn't much difference between the story to the people through film and bringing people to the story via safaris. We still had our tourism contacts in the parks and of course had our own marketable backgrounds- especially Julie with her parents and childhood. This was a more enjoyable use of our time. *Outside* magazine rated us as one of "The Best 35 Trips of the Year".

At one point I thought about getting my MBA. I took the GMATs and scored in the 88th percentile. On my very first day of class, Julie and I again had the chance to return to Africa to wrap up a film Des and Jen had been working on for several years. Answering the call of the wild once more, we took off for Namibia. Again, this was the right move.

Des and Jen were living in a small cabin in the Skeleton Coast Park, remotely situated three-hundred miles from anyone else, on the coast of the Atlantic Ocean. With a cold 42-degree (Fahrenheit) current coming up from Antarctica and the oldest desert in the world, a constant 22-knot southwesterly wind blew some of the largest sand dunes into existence, up to one thousand feet. It also provided a constant and cool-to-comfortable temperature band several miles wide along the coast. As we settled ourselves into the cabin and discussed the needs of the film, I discovered that National Geographic had sent an audio team over to try and record the strange sound of what the locals called "roaring dunes".

The sand dunes in Namibia are approximately inclined at 16-degrees on their "front", the side facing the constant wind off the Atlantic Ocean, and 32-degrees on the back. Due to the specific mineral composition of the desert, sometimes the wind would cause a cascade of sand over the top of a dune and down the back. As the particles picked up speed, they would cause more grains of sand on the leeward side to begin to slide and tumble. This cascade would create a harmonic of low moaning, then roaring, sound. Imagine the distant of a squadron of WW2 bombers flying overhead and you have the idea. The audio team couldn't get a good recording and they weren't able to figure out how to record it.

One day I was sitting on the backside of a dune, just thinking about it. I'm not sure where the inspiration came from, but I reviewed the technical specifications of our different microphones and studied the wave print of the frequencies they were tuned to. For two of the microphones I saw what looked like an opportune overlap of high and low frequencies that might capture the ranges created by the dunes. I connected the two microphones to the two channels of audio, tried it, made some adjustments and it worked. The result has to be one of the more unusual categories for an Emmy, especially for a National Geographic Television Special. But I'll take it.

***

It was around this time that the meeting with Disney on the sand dune took place. To this day, I think of this of this as one of the strangest synchronicities in my life, one in which another childhood dream came true. Fascinated by Disney as a child and the Disney-esque visions of the future in *Popular Mechanics* magazine, what more poetic or perfect Sign than to have a Disney film crew find my exact position in the middle of nowhere, demonstrate the use some exotic satellite telephone technology, and fire my imagination in such a way I then went to create what I did - a "Satellite TV Truck in a Backpack." If that wouldn't have been a vision of the future in the 1960s, I don't know what would be.

After I saw the first satellite telephone, my brain was on fire with my crazy idea: clear on the end result but fuzzy on how I'd get there, I flew back to the United States and met with the satellite telephone manufacturer and told them I wanted to transmit live video from the most remote and beautiful places in the world, directly into the internet. I could then share in real time the adventure of our lives in the bush with school kids all over the globe. They got onboard and gave me unlimited use of a satphone for over a year and all the $10/minute satellite time I could eat. Next, I went to Bell Labs and made friends there with Wendy

Hickey, who was very receptive to the idea. She provided me an analog desktop videophone that could plug into the sat-phone. In the initial meeting, some of the engineers pulled out their pads, performed some calculations and said it wouldn't work because the video modems of two video phones wouldn't stay in synch over the 22,500 miles up to the geostationary satellite then back again. I told them I had my system in the car and we could test it out right then. *And it worked.* They then asked how they could help me- so they gave me a videophone and lots of remote assistance. Wendy and I remain in touch to this day, and she's seen the fruit of her belief take form and reach goals neither of us at the time could have imagined.

***

I returned to Africa and tested this prototype system numerous times with Bell Labs. We had intermittent success but also had some challenges resulting from the fact that the transmission of video and audio signals were analog. This meant they did not have the superior error-correction of a digital signal needed to handle all the variables being throwing at it. We would have to wait another year or two until the digital satellites were launched.

Around this time, Julie and I divorced and parted as friends, which we still are.

Returning to America with little else than my prototype satellite system and my vision for how it would work, I reverse engineered the production process from what *would be* to what we could do now. I could have live audio with no problem. I could connect to the internet and that worked fine, it was just the criticality of sending live video that wasn't reliable at that time. I could edit and zip up video clips from my camera to my computer, connect my computer to the internet through the satphone, and send in nearly real time from anywhere I could hit a satellite. I then posted daily journal entries to wrap around the still and video images to share my adventure.

Doing just this, Microsoft hired me to retrace the Journey of the Magi through Iran, Syria, Jordan and Israel, where my team and I put together daily packages of our expedition for the Mungo Park website. Then it was to "Bush School" in Africa to share bushcraft lessons with kids on how to survive in the bush and then more trips to the Arctic and Antarctic. Adding my production with this technology to an IMAX film on Humpback whales in Maui for a month was great and helped promote in advance the making of the film. Eventually, my path led to the doorsteps of Yale University School of Medicine, where a new surgeon had arrived, Dr. (and Colonel) Rick Satava. He had just left his post, as the Director of Advanced Biological and Medical Projects (DARPA) and wanted to commercialize some of the technology he had funded in moving it from a classified to commercial status, so he brought the NASA Space Commercialization Center with him.

I had just been to Everest the year before with my system for the King of Malaysia, and proposed we go back to Everest to test some of the sci-fi medical technologies destined for the International Space Station. The thin air and rugged environment there would provide an interesting baseline to measuring the well-being of the climbers, especially in a place where your body is redlining even on a good day (you burn 4,000 calories/day just sitting at Everest Base Camp, at 17,500 feet altitude). The Head of Surgery made me a Lecturer in Experimental Surgery & Anatomy and Rick made me a NASA Principal Investigator. I began integrating the small medical monitoring devices into my satellite system. We even had a pill you could swallow that transmitted your internal body temperature for a radius of approximately one meter. A lightweight harness was designed with other biometrics built in- oxygen saturation of the blood, GPS, and so on. With the May climb window approaching, we quickly put our team and gear together and were ready .

We went two years in a row, the first year to articulate our questions and the second year to answer them. We also had a humanitarian mission, pausing in villages along the way to Everest Base Camp to render medical aid to the locals. I thank Drs. Ken Kamler, Jen Greshak and Chris Macedonia for that.

The missions were short term, successful and the updated gear was sent to the ISS. I went back to Everest two more times - five in succession – for more commercial ventures.

It was while up there in the rarefied air, half of what we have at sea level to breathe, that I discovered my knack for "feeling" satellite signals. I know that sounds weird, but I think it may be like dowsing, using a gut feel. It was when we were staying on the grounds of Thyengboche, a Tibetan monastery near the Chinese border, that we set up someone else's large satellite system with a dish antenna nine feet across. When it was time to aim it to the appropriate satellite, I asked the engineer if I could try and do it by feel. He said okay and watched his spectrum analyzer for the desired signal to appear on his screen if I nailed it. I stood in front of the dish with both hands on either side and first adjusted the elevation (up-down angle) to about 45-degrees. Then I slowly swept the sky with my back to it, my front to the dish. When I sensed the signal to be strongest, I stopped, then re-adjusted the elevation similarly, feeling for the signal to become stronger. When I went past that point, I then brought it back until I felt I had properly bracketed the main axis of the signal. A few minutes later, I asked the engineer if I was successful. He informed me that I was only 1.5-degrees off axis. 1 degree is about a finger's width. And this is all pre-near-death-experience (NDE).

Finally, the dot-com bubble burst. I could sense it coming during my last trip to Everest. On my way out, a synchronicity occurred. I was asked to report to NBC News by a highly placed friend of mine. There was a doctor at the South Pole who was being medevacked out and they wanted me to bring my system out ahead of the other news agencies to get the video and news first. I flew back to the USA from Kathmandu and hardly needed to repack, as where I was going as cold as where I'd been. I headed south to Punta Arenas, Chile to meet the rest of the team.

Upon arrival, I was informed that by good fortune the flight crew bringing the doctor out had seized upon an opportune weather window and we would not ourselves need to go to Antarctica- so we setup operations in Punta Arenas to do everything we needed there in anticipation of the flight's arrival to us. Other news agencies were arriving with their own satellite telephones, but none had the video components I had assembled to take full advantage. Up on the roof of the hotel, I walked around with my new satellite telephone, now the size of a laptop computer and aimed my antenna in the main direction of the satellite. As we were so far south, the satellites were lower to the horizon and more of the atmosphere ate up more of their energy. The other news crews, knowing who I was, followed me around the roof, hoping to get a usable signal of their own. Because of my corporate sponsorship that helped me be first-to-market, I made a call to Inmarsat and they steered an Atlantic West satellite toward me so I could have a better signal. It leaked out what I'd done, which increased my street cred considerably. It pays to have connections!

Upon return, I went into NBC News field operations and met with Stacy Brady, the VP of Field Operations, to further discuss using the system in new and innovative ways, providing advantages over competing networks. Within the week, they made an offer to hire me, that offer being received and discussed over my satellite phone while I was diving in Puerto Rico- after all, I was in need of a real holiday.

It was about that time I got a phone call from the Pentagon, based on their interest in my system, which I'd just demonstrated on the fantail of an aircraft carrier in the Persian Gulf for CNN. While jets took off and landed above me, other ships in the area were firing cruise missiles at Iraq.

On the fantail, I setup two satellite phones, having hacked the bonding code of the communications board, allowing me to split the video signal up into two separate satellite signals. This is called inverse-multiplexing and is used to add together multiple satellite signals to increase the size of the transmission pipeline of video and therefore its quality. I sent one signal up to a satellite over the Atlantic Ocean and the other signal to one over the Indian Ocean. The Atlantic Ocean satellite then connected to a Land Earth Station in Norway and the Indian Ocean satellite signal went down to a station in Malaysia. Then the two signals traveled terrestrially to the destination endpoint at CNN in Atlanta and re-bonded to become a viewable live video signal. This required that through all those crazy paths, the two signals would each travel in opposite directions halfway around the world and meet to re-connect within 1.5 seconds of each other.

The Pentagon invited me to come to DC to have lunch. It was a great meeting and several things were offered, of which one was a phone number for me to call if I ever got into trouble, with the promise I would be extracted within 24 hours.

My relationship with the military grew, as did my role at NBC News. When 9-11 occurred, I'd been there exactly three months, and left immediately for another three months. First, to the UK bureau to build more systems like mine for other teams to use, then down to Egypt because America was about to go in and bomb the snot out of every known and suspected terrorist training camp in northern Africa. Later I was redirected to Uzbekistan and Tajikistan, where I picked up some things to take across the border into Afghanistan. "Passport Control" was some guy sitting in a tent and wrapped in a shawl who looked at my passport and said wryly, "Welcome to Afghanistan". A line out of a movie, right?

I spent three months in Afghanistan, eventually driving through the Hindu Kush and into Kabul, where many people were literally camping in the Intercontinental Hotel. It had no power and barely running water. Some of us went and found a house in a neighborhood to rent. But word got out and suddenly more people showed up than the house could hold, so I bailed on this and went back to the hotel. The next morning the rest of the crew showed up with their gear and explained that an unexploded 500 lb. bomb dropped by "us" was found in the pantry, nose into the dirt and just waiting to detonate. They said I was lucky I left and I casually joked, to their strange looks, "God protects the righteous."

I soon went to the Philippines and Indonesia to partner up with their Special Forces and chase Abu Sayyaf terrorists. We did that for several weeks. During that time, I further hacked the satellite transmission bonding code on one of the boards I had installed in my computer to handle four different satellite signals and then I asked the Army to make a small hole in the jungle canopy by using the branches between the satellite and me for target practice. As at Everest, I could feel (dowse?) where the satellite was and I was able to connect to it once the branches were removed. From there and like that, my team hosted a one-hour news special, tossing to other teams all around the world and returning to where we were in the jungle. At the same time, I was being interviewed by Wired magazine and continually yelling at the military personnel to not walk in front of the satellite dishes. It was a fun time.

Then I returned home and took the rest of the year off. Everyone knew we were preparing to invade Iraq, so I talked to the other news agencies to determine which one I wanted to go with- I had a good relationship with key people at each one. It was at this time I met my wife, Dana, and her three babies. In February of the following year, I had to go down to the forests outside Washington, DC for some specialized training by the SAS (British Special Forces). I deployed overseas to Kuwait and was embedded with the Blue Knights Marine helicopter squadron out of Wilmington, NC. We were in the initial assault and for the next week, I remained with them. Then General Joe Kelly put me on his helicopter and flew me to the tip of the spear, where I was re-embedded with the First Battalion, Fourth Marines.

In short order, we saw action including the Battle of Al Kut, were later artilleried by our own side in the middle of the night and eventually rolled into Baghdad. Our Armored Personnel Carriers crossed a river and we took over a dump, sleeping in the dirt that night. Then we invaded a sewage plant, again sleeping in the dirt while Humvees, APCs and tanks drove around stirring up all kinds of dust with God-knows-what in it. Finally, we took over a cigarette factory in the town's outskirts, as it had a large protective wall around it and a tall tower we could use for observation.

A few days later Dana told me that her aunt, a nun in the Missionaries of Charity (founded by Mother Teresa), reported that no one in her Order had heard from their enclave of Sisters in Baghdad since the bombing had ended. She wondered if I could find out anything. I went to the Colonel whose Battalion I was embedded with and asked him. He went to Marine Intelligence who in turn went to the CIA and repeated the request. They had no intel but gave us the grid- the location, of where the nuns were. The Colonel armed me and gave me the use of an armored Humvee and 3 men to go find the nuns. We drove alone and fast through the unsecured city, jumping lane dividers and curbs, with the machine gunner leveling his big turret mounted gun to stop traffic. One of the Marines kept calling out our GPS coordinates and the driver turned right, then left, barreling down the chaotic streets to grid's address. Finally, we pulled up to a row of residences and stopped. I disarmed myself and pulled off my helmet and body armor so I wouldn't scare the nuns. There was a sign that told us we'd found our mark over the door.

*In front of the Missionaries of Charity, Baghdad, Iraq, April 18, 2003*

I knocked on the door and a nun answered, wearing Birkenstocks. She was Bangladeshi and had a very chill vibe. Friendly but unflustered, she answered the door and treated me with a smile and an aura of peacefulness. I explained why I was there, that no one had heard from her order since the invasion. She told me they were fine and invited me inside. I turned to my team and gave them the thumbs up and with another hand signal, that I was going inside and to wait.

I went in and saw a simple but tidy home. I met three other nuns; two more from Bangladesh and one from India. I introduced myself as a reporter from NBC News in America and asked why they hadn't left when the bombing started. The nun who let me in beckoned me into another room, where I saw over 20 cribs with infants. She waved at them and asked me where they would have gone. Then I saw that *every* one of the children had severe handicaps of one sort or another. Many were mentally challenged, another had flippers for arms and legs. And so on. There was no way these few women could have evacuated everyone with the resources they had.

I asked about the kids and she said they had all been left at their door by parents who didn't want them. Yet they were clean, well fed and appeared happy. I was taken aback and asked if I could interview and film them for a story. Their natural inclination of humility responded "no". I thought for a moment, understanding, then said the story wasn't to glorify their efforts, but to share their example of sacrifice, something the world needed to see. They discussed it for a few minutes then said okay. I asked it was alright if I invited in my team and they agreed.

They came in and it was wonderful to see them not as the war-hardened Marines, but as men who have children or younger brothers and sisters. They held the babies, bounced them up and down and it was obvious how needed this moment of tenderness was. As I interviewed the nuns one at a time, the others showed my team around, all the while still carrying babies. I went out and got one of my sat-phones and set it up and told the sisters to call whoever was important to them and tell them they were okay. I dialed in the satellite access digits then the phone numbers they gave me. We wrapped up with a promise to soon return and check on them again.

We returned to the cigarette plant we took possession of and I edited the footage and uplinked it to NBC in New York. We aired it on Good Friday and I was on air with this as my first story. It aired at least ten more times over Easter weekend. Then a couple of Humvees went over to the bombed out local UN offices and grabbed bolts of fabric, electrical cord, light bulbs and anything else of value and returned. My team organized a bunch of Humanitarian Rations- they are like MREs (Meals Ready to Eat; think battlefield rations) but in a yellow identifying pouch- to be put into a couple of other Humvees. We drove our caravan back to the Mission and unloaded it all inside their convent. As two of the nuns reviewed the inventory from the UN, two more opened up the rations and began cooking them. The Marines laughed and told them they could prepare them that way, but there are built in flameless, chemical heaters that when you add water, heat the food instead. All in all, it seemed as much an opportunity to do some good as it was for additional Marines to come and hold babies. It was a very human moment.

The next day, a few of the Marines got upset stomachs, and so did I. We figured it was from sleeping on the ground in the sewage plant and garbage dump on our way in. A Navy doctor assigned to us- a really great guy- gave me some medicine then offered to knock me out so that I could rest and let the meds do their work. He gave me a shot and I unrolled my mat and went to sleep on the ground within the confines of the cigarette factory. I have no idea when I went to sleep but it must have been only minutes after. When I awoke a few hours later, there was a huge M1-A1 Abrams tank parked only inches from my head. In jest, the tank must have pulled in with the idea that I would wake up at some point when they pulled in, startled. I can only imagine what they thought when I didn't. But I got the joke and thought it funny, nonetheless.

I shot, produced and aired some more stories for NBC News and then as the Army showed up, we handed off to them and went south 60 miles to Hillah, or by its ancient name, Babylon. We walked around the ruins Saddam had recently added to in celebration of Iraqi glory from millennia ago. On many of the bricks were propaganda statements for Hussein, all *glorifyingly* inaccurate. Even so, it was still interesting to see the ancient buildings. I even did a story on the place. Some of the ruins were in the final stages of decay, the mud bricks being reclaimed by the earth with only their sharp 90-degree edges and corners giving away they were anything but the dirt they came from, formed by hands ages and ages ago.

NBC decided it was time for me to leave and I waited in an adjacent open area for a CH-46 helicopter to pick me up. I was surprised and honored by the large group of Marines who came out to see me off. We laughed at the times I would setup my sat-phone on my Humvee and loudly announce that I was going to take a walk. I would return an hour later to see more candy than I could ever eat left on the phone, pulled from military rations (MREs), in thanks for allowing some of the guys to speak to their wives who had borne their children while here, to aging parents who buried one or the other during this time, or to spouses trying to hold shaky marriages together.

The helicopter finally arrived and I walked into the back and dropped my kit. I transferred my weapons back to the unit (the ones I officially didn't have) and we shook hands and hugged goodbye. Then we took off for Kuwait.

We flew at high altitude to avoid any ground fire issues and as we approached Al Nasiriyah, to the south, we began experiencing hydraulic failure. We put down in a field next to the base the Army had setup there and while the pilots called in the situation to get either a new part of a new helicopter, I went inside the base. In the PX, I saw an American flag hanging up behind the register and asked if I could buy it; so I did. That is the only American flag I have and I still fly it on holidays. That evening, we ate with some of the teams on the base, then went back out to the field near the CH-46 and setup our tents. It was decided that another helicopter would pick us up and we would carry on to Ali Al Saleem air base on the Kuwait border. We broke and tied infrared light sticks to our tents - like those you see used at Halloween to light up roving trick or treaters -- except you couldn't see these in action unless you had infrared or night vision goggles. This allowed us to avoid being seen by anyone who would cause trouble. I cut a small portion off a block of C-4 explosive, took out my cigar torch and lit the block on fire to boil water for us, adding in the instant coffee from our MREs. It's funny to think that you can use an explosive like C-4 to make coffee. It needs both pressure and heat to explode. I could boil a metal cup of water in 90 seconds, stir the coffee in, then transfer it to a cooler cup so you didn't cauterize your lips to it when you drank.

At some point in the night, we heard a helicopter coming in and lit new night sticks, to make sure we were seen and they wouldn't blow us all across the field by landing too close to the tents. Once they were on the ground, we quickly packed up our stuff and boarded. We flew home in the dark and safely landed in Kuwait. I slept a couple more nights on the base, saying goodbye and thank you to the Marines in the helicopter squadron I was originally embedded with. We even dressed normally one day and went into Kuwait City to eat lunch and shop around. I flew on a commercial airliner home.

Dana and the three kids met me at JFK in a limo and gave me a hero's welcome. Within the week, we all went to Disney World to kick the summer off properly. Already, NBC was making plans to send me back, so we stayed in touch during the vacation. Upon return, Dana and I went into New York City to an NBC party, where all the correspondents were and she got to meet them all in person. It really was like a family. A video had been put together of all of our highlights during the war and everyone was recognized in it. I rounded out my part in the event as a guest on one of Lester Holt's shows, where he interviewed me for a behind the scenes view of my time there.

Summer passed and I thought of changing jobs. I had enjoyed my time in the war but being home, I liked having a family. When we went to church, the Priest (Father Bob), was very excited about Dana's and my union and came down into the congregation, asked me to stand and thanked God in front of everyone that I'd returned safely. The entire congregation knew Dana and the kids, many attending both her wedding with her deceased husband and not long after his funeral. They were concerned about the prospects of a widow with three babies. With the Priest's blessing, the entire church started clapping so loudly that I awkwardly waved, bowing thanks to them all, then sat down. What do you say to that?

I also thought that while I might be happy dashing off to war, it wasn't fair to the children- to risk losing someone who was becoming their father. That kind of trauma might be too much to bear. I began looking at how I could translate my experience with digital media technology to a corporate environment.

I found a position at a large pharmaceutical company an hour away and applied for it. I was able to have a quick interview before leaving for Iraq in August. For the next few months, I stayed in touch with them and continued the interview process, even at that distance.

When I arrived in Baghdad, I found my NBC News team in a hotel. They had taken over several rooms and created a makeshift production newsroom. At this time, the need to embed with the military wasn't there, as the main focus now was rebuilding Iraq and embracing the future. As soon as possible, it was thought, the USA wanted to get out. Paul Bremmer, the head of the Provisional Authority, signed out as soon as he could and left, never to be heard from again. But not before he disbanded the entire Iraqi military, leaving a lot of angry, disenfranchised citizens with less to lose than before.

At the end of August, a bomb went off at a mosque in Najaf, several hours south of Baghdad. I went down there to check things out, with a local driver and translator. Once onsite, I walked casually through the throng to the mosque and took in the damage. Around seventy-five people were killed. In a few minutes, I saw that my presence was noticed and the feeling of the crowd was like a hornet's nest that had been knocked out of a tree. I turned and walked back to my waiting driver, with a growing crowd following me. They were also becoming more vocal, not appreciating my presence.

The closer I got to the car, the more I calculated the time it would take me to cover the remaining distance should I have to run. When I finally got to the car, the translator got out, leaving me the door open to enter as he tried to talk to the crowd. In an instant, they pulled him into the crowd and I shut my door. The crowd forced open the door and tried to pull me out. Fortunately, as it was hot summer in Iraq, I was wearing a lightweight shirt essentially made of gauze. One of my sleeves ripped in my assail-ants' hands and the way he looked up at me was strange- there was no anger, just a calm look of confusion. I didn't feel anger, or fear really, either. It was like we were there, both dispassionately playing our roles.

The driver yelled, the translator was still missing, so I jumped back in and he gunned the car out of there. Suddenly a sword flew in through the back window, shattering me with safety glass. I guess that sword might have been meant for me if I'd stayed with the crowd and this was their parting gift. We got out of there quickly and the crowd was really angry at their prey getting away. When we were several miles away, the driver stopped, I think to breathe. We got out and he asked me for my shirt. I took it off and gave it to him. He took out his knife and cut the other sleeve off, saying that it now had the right look. I wish I'd kept the sword, but I did keep the shirt.

*Wearing my torn-up shirt from Najaf, Iraq, August 2003*

We were unable to do anything for our translator. We returned to our hotel/news bureau in Baghdad and debriefed everyone. The next day our translator turned up, and we were greatly relieved, as there were no police to report the incident to and the US military wasn't about to get involved in such local matters. We ate a dinner together in gratitude. The next day, I heard that more crew members were arriving and the hotel was filling up beyond capacity. I volunteered to go around the corner and down the street to a neighboring hotel.

That night, someone set off a bomb at the hotel I'd just left, right under my window. Some of the locals who worked at the hotel slept in the lobby at night and were killed. No news personnel were harmed but the room I had stayed in- which was empty and awaiting its new occupant- was blown all to hell. I can't say if I would have died or not, but I'm just as happy to remain ignorant of the certainty in that regard.

The news team immediately jumped on the event as a story, as well as pulled out to another hotel that was more defensible. The new teams arriving didn't even unpack their bags and were already schlepping to the new hotel. Indeed, it was much better in every way, and further out from the center of town.

As all the equipment was moved into the new place, I revisited the nearby Army base, had them check my credentials and was issued an MP5 with no serial number, a 9mm Iraqi knock off of a Beretta and what passed for a 6.5mm (tiny) Saturday Night Special from the Czech Republic- I kept that in my sock. I was carrying again but was 24/7 with news crews. If I ever pulled anything out, it would be a one-way trip either in life or profession. I would only draw my weapons if there was a danger to my life or someone I needed to protect but if any news personnel were present, my journalism days would be over- journalists don't carry weapons and in fact count on everyone knowing that and sparing their lives during a firefight. I knew that was BS and it was proven several times.

One day I went into the Baghdad Hunting Club, ate lunch, "made friends" and went shooting with them in the desert at dawn the next day. I don't know why I was inspired to do this. I went inside, ordered lunch and looked around to see who was noticing me. I saw a corner table of older gentlemen who had some polish to them. They occasionally glanced at me. I acknowledged them with a nod and eventually we began talking.

They were high up Iraqi Air Force officers that we had put out of business. They appeared to enjoy alcohol, a lot of it. We eventually were swapping jokes and laughing. They invited me to go shooting with them the next morning. I said okay. We agreed on a place they would pick me up.

That afternoon I pulled a couple of security guys aside and told them they would be going with me. Then I loaded up my guns and went to bed early.

The next morning some nice, new large SUVs pulled up and my guys and I simply followed them. We went about 90 minutes out into the desert, to where if they shot us no one would ever find us. We got out and shot at stuff. One of them had a nice Beretta hunting shotgun with the camo painted all over it, including the barrel but damn, he was the worst shot ever. It was hard clay-like soil with a few small canals crisscrossing through it. Suddenly, a kingfisher flew up and hovered over the water in a canal next to us and one of the Colonels took aim with the shotgun. I thought it terribly unsportsmanlike, but it was his karma, not mine. He pulled the trigger, rocked back with its kick…and clearly missed the bird. I think he was already drunk. Once the sun rose a little more and it went from warm to hot, we decided to call it quits. My security detail looked relieved this was over. I wasn't worried about anything bad happening to us.

The search for Saddam took me north to Tikrit, where he was originally from. It was thought that on the run, he would find Baath sympathizers in the area who would aid or hide him. I stayed in Saddam's palace on the Euphrates River; joined by a large contingent of the US Army. When they weren't talking to locals or following up on possible leads, they went on raids, throwing families out of their homes as they looked for the manufacture of IEDs: Improvised Explosive Devices.

These homemade explosives were the bane of everyone, using old mortar shells filled with explosives and remotely triggered with cell phones or even garage door openers. The IEDs could be buried in the ground next to the road or tucked into dead animals or road kills. When a car drove by, the detonator would be triggered and as many cars as could be destroyed would be. Many people died or were injured this way. I saw some horrifically torn up Humvees and it was a miracle that anyone survived. Many soldiers removed their body armor and sat on it as a form of protection.

Speaking of the nightly raids, the Army would go into neighborhoods and force men to wait outside at the front of their homes while women were made to wait out back. The soldiers then went through their homes looking for bomb making materials. I can't say how often they found it, but I believe it to be in a minority of cases. Of course, it only takes one to have a really bad day. But after going along and seeing how the guy leading them was a bit of a camera hog, I quickly lost my appetite for this activity. Oddly, I wondered if I had a premonition of seeing such a thing occurring in America one day. Now more than ever, I feel certainty in that.

In between journalism during the day and running around with the Army at night, I would take my lunch on the large terrace overlooking the river. I would read from the *Book of Mirdad* by Mikhail Naimy, a Lebanese writer and friend of Kahlil Gibran's. I also kept up correspondence with the pharmaceutical company, indicating my continued interest. Interest there was heating up and several things were coming together to bring me back home in October for one week: Follow-up interviews with the company and my girlfriend: I wanted to celebrate her birthday that week and get engaged.

Like a surgical strike mission, I flew home from Iraq to pick out a diamond in the Diamond District in New York City, to celebrate my new fiancé's birthday, to have several interviews with Big Pharma to report in at NBC News and then return to Baghdad. About as whirlwind a week as you can imagine.

During my interview with one Director at the pharma company, she asked if I would be happy giving up my exciting life in exchange for a corporate one with an office and little travel. Without hesitation, I told her that I don't look for happiness from my job. I look for fulfillment. Happiness is what I would expect from my family and not being on the other side of the planet and having a home to return to after 5:00pm would allow me exactly that. She smiled, closed her notebook and said, "That is exactly the answer. This interview is so out of the box that I'm not going to take notes". Within the month, they formalized their offer and I counted the days until I returned home, to my new life.

I said my goodbyes and returned my MP5 with no serial number, an Iraqi copy of a 9mm Beretta and a Czech 6.5 mm Saturday Night Special. These had been my constant companions.

*My Weapons Card, issued by the US Army*

*Heckler & Koch MP5 9mm machine gun*

*Tariq 9mm handgun, Beretta knockoff*

*VZOR 7mm handgun, "Saturday Night Special"*

Just before I left, I was in the Green Zone one day and Donald Rumsfeld surprisingly showed up- I was stuck there with a film camera, my 9mm pistol hidden in my flight suit and two metal detectors to walk through before going into the boardroom to interview him. I knew I was in a pickle only because of all the news crews suddenly around me and the "rule" that journalists don't carry guns. Well, not all of them are doing double duty either. I thought that I could get through the first detector by playing stupid and absent-mindedly walking with my camera through the first one but wasn't sure how to handle the second one. This went according to plan and when I triggered the first, the Army looked confused and with heightened awareness, motioned me to the second metal detector. Again, I had authorization from the military to carry, but not my news employer. Just as I began to walk toward the detector, Rumsfeld walked up and said, "Let him through" and they did so without question and without me going through the detector. It's an easy guess as to why he did this but I'll allow the reader their conjecture.

Once we were all assembled in the interview room, Rumsfeld's aides paid out the rules- everyone would get 90 seconds to interview him and all cameras were to point to the floor while he put on a bit of makeup for the lights- which everyone on camera used. The correspondent I was working with at the time and I got the first interview slot. We began the interview and I framed the shot in the camera. At around 60 seconds, I realized I hadn't hit "record" and panicked. When we were done, I had no choice but to say that and apologize, looking right into Rumsfeld's eyes. The correspondent was livid but said nothing as there were no second chances and every other network than ours would now have an interview for their evening news. The room gasped, waiting to see if he would rip me a new one. Then Rumsfeld said, "It's not like I've never made a mistake" and we did it again. Quite a day.

I flew by Blackhawk up to Kurdistan and got to know those folks- ran with the Peshmerga (Kurdish militia) in the surrounding hills- one made an apology for slowing me down because of the AK-47 round in his leg. I loved those people. Spent a little time with Qubad Talabani, whose father, Jalal Talabani, would go on to become president of Iraq. Overall though, I liked Kurdistan a lot. I feel badly for the terrible time they've had with almost every country they've lived in, and for their recent setbacks in fighting the Islamic State with the US pulling back its aid. When I was the Kurds, I felt like I was with my tribe- I considered moving back there with my family.

Finally, my time in Iraq drew to a close and with my new career awaiting me in the New Year, I flew home for the end of year holidays, picking up my son in the UK and we all spent Christmas and New Years with my fiancé's father and stepmother in Jupiter, FL. It was one of the best Christmases ever.

Returning home, I put my son on a flight and he returned to the UK and I tried on for size the clothing of a corporate animal. I was there for four years and the entire time I felt like I was under-cover, as it was most certainly not who I am. But I was grateful, as I said during my interview, for the opportunity to have a personal life and a family. My fiancé and I married in the spring and it was shortly after that she encouraged me to build my first aircraft, a WW1-era fighter, a plane that helped me transition from the War Jim to the New Jim. I always felt that I may have had unfinished business with this particular aircraft from a past life.

The rest of my corporate life took me on the scenic route through UNICEF as the technical director of all media, Ernst & Young as the global lead for voice and video telecommunications and then the shortest and worst decision I ever made, as a Director at HBO. It was a fiasco from the start. The difference between the job I interviewed for and the job I got was the exact difference between success and failure. Because of internal politics, my job title changed so much, along with the scope of my duties, that they kept canceling my business cards and not telling me. Eventually I told my "boss" that he needed a pair of balls to do his job and he fired me, to which my wife said, "Thank God you're out of that Hell Hole". Honestly, I preferred Iraq.

I took time off to reflect and met some of the most interesting people in my life. They were full of encouragement, expanding my network of new friendships and we considered all manner of new opportunities. I was encouraged to write about my experiences, tried, but eventually paused as I didn't want to be the center of one of "those" macho stories, arms crossed on the cover of *Men's Journal* magazine and looking available to deflower virgins by the dozens.

It took a while to come to that realization, nurtured by some rejections from Hollywood. They were interested in my story, but as I'm no screenwriter, I didn't have a script to follow-up with. It led to a stalemate for next steps.

It helped that I found a new line of work that suited me at the time- IT project management. There were short term assignments and I could manage different types of projects for multiple customers...perfect for someone with ADHD.

\*\*\*

I introduced you to Dana and her three babies and told you how they grew on me, enough that I changed course, married her and retired from the war business. I called this "The Day I Joined the Circus". Wanting to help me settle in, Dana suggested I build an airplane I'd been fascinated with since childhood.

I built my replica 1917 Fokker Triplane like the Red Baron flew, with my own paint scheme of black and white stripes. It was different to fly and with the powerful rudder and lift of three wings, if you weren't careful you could almost fly sideways. It flew well enough, requiring only constant control inputs due to its inherent instability, but it was totally manageable as long as you paid attention.

I learned this on the first day I flew it, which was totally unplanned. I thought I would gain confidence by doing some high-speed taxis down the field, getting the tail up, essentially flying it on the ground. Instead, as soon as I threw the throttle (pushed it all the way forward), the torque of the engine expressed through the long propeller, and the relatively short fuselage, caused the aircraft to whip toward the side and in thirty feet, the tail was up and picking up speed.

Due to my inexperience with the large rudder (an old saying among pilots of this aircraft is "The Rudder is God"), I over-corrected and the plane whipped back the other way, so I over-corrected again, all the while building up speed. Somehow, I had the presence of mind to realize that the only way to save it was to pull back on the stick and fly it. Both the trees bordering the airstrip and a row of planes tied down along it was fast approaching. With a pucker factor of 10, I pulled back to see what would happen next. To my surprise, the Triplane lifted off!

Now I was in an environment where I was used to operating an aircraft. The plane rose up into the sky and I looked down at the ground distancing itself from me, and I looked at the black and white stripes of the wings against the background of the landing field, somehow reminiscing about all the time I spent designing, measuring and painting them.

I snapped back to the business of flying and what I would do next. One problem I'd not accounted for was that I had not yet tuned the carburetor. As a result, black smoke was coming out of the exhaust pipes. I didn't know it, and my friends on the ground were very concerned. Before I made my first turn, I suddenly felt a hard, constant blast of air on my right cheek and wondered what that was all about. I looked down to my bank indicator and it became apparent I was pointing 45-degrees off my axis of travel: I was flying sideways!

One day, I decided to push it past cruising to its top speed of just over 100-knots, the same speed you would reach when entering an aerial battle.

At the DR-1's top speed, its personality totally changes. You feel like you're riding along the edge of a razor blade with the throttle wide open, and the slightest control input have instant and powerful results- you could suddenly whip into a turn before any enemy could react. You ran as much risk of giving yourself whiplash as taking an enemy round from their machine guns. Being distracted for even a moment was not an option. What was once a winged horse was now a dragon. Aerial battle in WW1 must have been terrifying on every level.

My hero was Werner Voss, who on September 23, 1917, took on a crack squadron from the British Royal Air Force. One against seven, his machine guns put rounds in all of them to the point none of the aircraft could fly again. Finally, he ran out of gas and was a sitting duck. RAF combatants said how much they hated shooting him down, as they had never seen such skill or bravery before. Had he lived, his record might have surpassed his friend and rival, Manfred von Richtofen, the Red Baron- who had a total of 81 kills- the highest in the war. In honor of his memory, I made the aircraft number 239/17 and the other number 1956. My birthday is 23-9-1956, more encouraging my affinity with the man and the aircraft.

*Lt. Werner Voss in a fight with 7 SE5a's, September 23, 1917*

*My reproduction 1917 Fokker DR1 Triplane, 2012*

I built my second aircraft, an improved copy of a 1933 French Flying Flea. Whimsical in design, it looked like a lot of fun. As with the DR-1, this is a design I fell in love with in my early teens. The creator of the HM-14 Flying Flea was Henri Mignet (French,

1893-1965). Mignet's desire was to design aircraft that were easy to build and fly and their size suggested that you could build them on your dining room table in a modest Paris apartment. Their engines were repurposed motorcycle engines. The skill to fly them was minimal due to the slow speed, light weight and ease of control. But as with the first DR-1s, flaws in the early models caused some deaths and hampered its wider adoption even as its popularity grew.

As with my DR-1, my N-number was meaningful, the date of Mignet's death – N83165.

*My reproduction 1933 HM-14 Flying Flea, 2016*

The Flying Flea's homebuilt movement invited experimentation and so there was no "standard model" after a short time. I incorporated an external landing gear with heavy duty springs for shock absorbers to account for my greater weight and my larger and more powerful BMW motorcycle engine. I added an extra rib section to both the upper and lower wings to add more lift against the extra weight. I had a beautiful handmade wooden propeller that said "vintage" as much as the paint scheme approximating the original. I put in minimal instrumentation as per regulations set by the Federal Aviation Administration and the same inspector who certificated my DR-1 returned with a new colleague to certify my Flea.

Awaiting perfect weather to test fly the aircraft, I heard of a nearby air show and got permission to bring my plane. Most people displaying aircraft flew in but I wasn't about to make my first test flight at an event. I folded its wings, put it on a U-Haul trailer and drove it to the airshow.

I got a trophy for most unusual design. Everyone loved the Flea's quirky look and it was fun to stand there like everyone else in the crowd as smiling people jockeyed for position to get the best selfie. Many came over and introduced themselves, inviting me to visit their hangars and see their projects. Some of their aircraft were way beyond the skill and expense of even my DR-1, so I was very flattered by their attention. I also had more hands than I could use to help offload the plane from the trailer and put it back on again, ending an airshow during a beautiful New England fall day in September.

I practiced many high-speed taxis and aborted takeoff runs in order to confidently feel I had control over that very small aircraft. In a plane this short and with no brakes, if I started to lose directional control, things would go badly quickly. I finalized the adjustments in the control linkages and for the first time pushed the throttle forward with the expectation of flying.

I could tell as soon as I'd crossed the speed threshold that felt like the point of no return. In my heart and mind, that signified full commitment. As soon as I felt the tail lift, I wanted to get off the ground and into what's called ground effect, a distance from the ground equal to half the wingspan. In that cushion of air, lift is increased, drag is reduced and the stall speed is lower. I could then build up speed to climb out- a preference over traveling faster while on the ground to build up more speed- things can get out of control very quickly in such a short aircraft. I pulled the stick back and muddled my way two or three feet off the ground. I needed to pick up speed, so I remained at this low altitude for a few more seconds until I felt the controls become smoother, indicating I had reached climb speed. I eased back on the stick and the BMW engine turning the big prop sounded great as it streaked into the sky at all of 65 mph.

When I reached the right altitude, I turned left to stay in the pattern around the airfield, meaning close enough to make it back to the grass strip should I lose power. On my downwind leg, I decided to add in a full 360-right hand turn. As soon as I began the turn, the plane felt like it wanted to flip over onto its back. I lessened pressure then added it back in smaller increments, determining the threshold of where that behavior became apparent, while making my turn in small pieces- start the turn, then back off. Start it again then back off. These increments would add up to 360-degrees in a minute or two. No matter if it presents a convoluted solution, a pilot needs to feel that he has control over making the aircraft go where he wants, even if it seems like a negotiation.

I went around a couple of times in the pattern, tried another 360 to confirm what I thought was true was indeed so, then set up for my final approach. As soon as I cleared the trees, I chopped throttle, and did the plane ever drop! I had read how its "dirty" aerodynamics meant its glide ratio was poor but as soon as I experienced it, I pushed the throttle forward as fast as I could. This helped a little and flattened the glide out somewhat, but I still hit the ground with a bounce. The beefed-up landing gear took it well and I kept my power on to stretch my distance and lessen the impact force of the second bounce. The lesson was that I'd have to come in faster and at a flatter angle, which meant not chopping the throttle, but flying the aircraft to the ground with the power on.

Overall, I was pleased- this was my first test flight in my second experimental aircraft and we were both in re-usable condition. I taxied back to the hangar, put it inside, stood for a moment looking at it proudly and then went home.

Three days later, on Thursday October 6th, I decided to go up again to master the Flea's quirks. I took off and noticed that when making a turn during a climb, the strange tendency to flip over wasn't apparent. I kept my turn going until I was in a position to fly down the length of the runway, and I could see a couple of my friends standing there watching. At the right time, I brought my throttle back slightly and started a turn to line me up with the center of the runaway.

I didn't want to land but execute a Touch & Go, where my wheels just kissed the ground and I would hit the throttle and fly again. On my final, though, I discovered a new strange trait of my plane; it was yawing back and forth. That's where it swivels left and right around its center of gravity and with my large rudder, I wondered if my efforts to stop the yawing might be creating a PIO, Pilot Induced Oscillation. To keep things from getting worse, I increased power. The oscillations stopped and again I rose into the sky. This time on my way back around, my engine suddenly stopped. Fortunately, I didn't panic, so I restarted the engine but it quit again. Due to the poor glide ratio of its vintage design and with only forested hills all around me, the one place I could aim for was a small lake in a nearby Boy Scout camp. There was just no way I would make it back to the airstrip. Trying to compensate for the steep rate of sink, I came in a little hotter than I needed to but successfully at a flatter glide ratio…and overshot the lake's shore by ten feet, crashing into the large tree trunks at water's edge.

*Scenes from my crash of the Flying Flea, north of Waterbury, CT, October 6, 2016*

When I stopped crashing, there was no aircraft left around me. Only the rear portion was intact, to which I was still seat-belted. A good Samaritan named Greg Gubitosi was fishing nearby and ran over to help. He called 911 and kept me propped up so I could gasp for air. I was unable to breathe normally and blood foamed from my mouth, sign of a ruptured lung. In fact, both lungs were ruptured, all my ribs were broken, my right leg looked like a pretzel, I had a hole in my lower back from where the aircraft engine's battery broke loose, becoming a projectile. The skin on my chin was shredded, making it impossible to form words without the use of my lower lip. Otherwise, I was fine. Half an hour later, LifeStar flew in to rescue me.

The helicopter crew cut my seatbelt and placed me on a gurney, rolled me across the ground and secured me in their aircraft. Greg became concerned as they sat there for more time than he would have thought an emergency allowed. My guess is they were stabilizing me and perhaps filling out forms. Once this was done, they took off for Hartford and to a waiting trauma team.

Please understand that I had to put this all together later, in speaking with Greg and the doctors.

I have no memory of the crash or two days prior. I looked through my emails to find one I recognized, so that's how I know when my memory ceased. I do remember seeing my propeller stop, restarting it and seeing it stop again. In revisiting my crash site a year later, I figured out my problem-solving process by noting where I was told I was when I lost my engine and the fact the water was a better place to aim, rather, than the forests and rocky hills.

A few hours later, my wife, the kids and a few friends stopped by. One brought my phone and it was plugged in next to me, not that I had immediate plans to use it. I was pumped up with pain killers, in a breathing machine, intubated with tubing coming into and going out of me from every imaginable place. I suffered acute respiratory failure. Once that emergency passed, I must have thought I was in an enemy hospital and about to be tortured, because I asked my oldest daughter to remove one of my restraints so I could scratch my face. She suspected my true motives and said no. I apparently relaxed, moving my arms in such a way as to escape one of my restraints. My daughter called for help which resulted in my only other memory during this time: angry orderlies entering the room with me thinking, "They're going to hurt me now."

This stunt created a conversation between the doctors and my wife. Being a handful and with a full week of six-plus hour operations needed, some with a small chance of success, they recommended to her that I be put into a coma for the duration. She agreed, and so they did.

From my family's side, the surgeons would discuss the operation required that day. My daughter said that they began the grieving process then as a couple of operations had a low survival rate, in one case, only two percent.

Part II:

# The In Between

*As the doctors put me into a medically induced coma here, I woke up somewhere else. I left my body and was in a purgatorial looking place I learned was called the In Between. In my later research, it sounds similar to the Tibetan Bardo, the Buddhist term for a liminal state between births. My guess is that you can color it in however you like. For my purposes it looked like New York, a thousand years after a nuclear blast or asteroid impact. Here is my account of what I came to understand was a Near-Death Experience (NDE).*

Chapter Two:

# The In Between

My vision comes into focus first on my right knee, then my left foot planted firmly on the ground. I look up and see that I am on the terrace of a tall building. It is open and everything is gray as if made of concrete and in ruins. Building upon building stretch into the distance, each partially destroyed but weaving together to create a post-apocalyptic skyline. There is no sound of any sort either. It's just that quiet. As I look up to the sky, I see clouds so dark and heavy with rain that their readiness to unload is imminent and frightening. Everything- the ruined buildings, the storm-ready sky, even the air itself seem to be waiting with the same tension as an arrow drawn tight on a mythical bow.

Suddenly a wave of nausea runs through my gut and even though I am kneeling, I double over in pain and grab my stomach. I whisper aloud, "I don't think I can stand this!"

With these words I sense something to my left. On the terrace not far away is one of the eeriest sculptures I have ever seen.

*The In Between*

Standing out against the darkest parts of the brooding sky is a large egg-shaped sculpture. It appears to be made of curved bands of metal, crisscrossing in what seems to be a random pattern but in the overall form of an egg standing on its end. I can also see small whirling patterns slow down within.

Still feeling my stomach gripped in pain, I rise to my feet and do my best to walk over to the monolith. As I look through the open lattice work, I can see the source of arcing patterns of movement- there are gears inside. They are freely suspended in space, but each anchored to an invisible and unique pivot point defining their sweeping arcs of movement in every different and imaginable direction. I notice that these are sector gears, the kind you see in clock-like mechanisms. In contrast to a round gear, these are only a small part of an entire toothed circle, therefore with a beginning, middle and end.

*Sector Gear*

As I watch the otherworldly dance of the gears, I can see that some are real and definite and others are ghostlike. They pass through each other without interference and I can hear the whisper of a light, clacking sound as they ratchet around inside the egg. I take a few steps back to take it all in.

"What *is* this thing?", I ask.

A disembodied VOICE responds within my consciousness.

*"This is the future birthing into the now."*

The otherworldly dance of the gears is complex, like a 4-D model of time. They come to rest and I reach through a gap in the side of the egg.

*This is the process of Becoming.*

As I look at the gears, within my mind I see something like a video feed of future events. One brushes my outstretched hand and suddenly I double over in pain.

With a reflex, I rip the gear out, pulling it through the egg's lattice wall and throw it over my shoulder. The machine responds by spinning its gears around again, recalibrating for the loss of one, whispering its light clacking sound into a new configuration.

"What's happening now?"

*Each gear is the probability of a thought, word or action in your future. Your destiny is resetting itself around what you have removed.*

"How did I know I could do that? Pull that gear out, removing that future moment?"

*Why else are you here?*

"I have no idea. I don't even know what this place is."

**You are in the In Between.**

"In between what?"

*Everything. The Impossible Now between the past and the future.*

"That makes no sense whatsoever."

*It's impossible in its short duration. Yet here you are, standing inside the eternity of a single moment. Do you remember who you are in the world to which your body belongs?*

I look blankly into space, squinting with the effort to remember.
"No."

*Then you see the truth in how the past is dust.*

"OK. Why do some of these gears- these *futures* that I touch- make me sick and not others?"

*All choices have unintended consequences, some unfortunate and some not. The pain each brings is your guide.*

"Where are the gears that feel good?"

*You're not here to feel good.*

A new gear swings into view. On this one I see a Ferris wheel and happy grandchildren whizzing by, fingers grasping their car, laughter... they smile at me, or through me, looking off into their own world.

Obviously, I let that gear pass by.

More gears emerge within view, some passing through others, several clear and definite, many less so and hard to focus on, though all bringing with them their clear images of meaning.

Each time they come to rest, I pull out a gear that I feel by my pain to be to my future detriment.

At one point I look at the growing pile of gears.

"It's starting to look like if I don't have a bad future then I have no future at all. Even though I now feel less pain, am I going to die sooner from doing all this?"

*Your destiny has to fit itself around futures that aren't meant to be. Your number of breaths are already counted. I will worry about your last one.*

"I don't know how comforting that is."

*Eliminating bad choices doesn't mean you won't make wrong ones. You won't know they are wrong until after they pass. Since right and wrong are variables over which you have no control, the answers to what comes tomorrow are a waste. Better is understanding the beauty of how everything fits and re-fits together.*

"So what am I missing here, in my lack of understanding?"

*What is clearly before you. Grace. No one deserves salvation- It can only be given by Grace. It is your birthright, but it must be chosen at the expense of the world that separates us.*

"This fixing my future is painful. I feel ashamed that I'm not doing it with some moral compass. I'm only guided by pain. I don't even know where or when these futures happen."

*Where or when are not important. Removing your enthusiasm to further chain yourself to the world isn't as painful as carrying the crushing weight of those chains, once forged around you.*

"It's as if this place was made so that I can do one thing and one thing only, with no chance to screw it up."

*If those with choices make poor use of them, then offering fewer possibilities could be called mercy.*

I watch a gear disintegrate into dust as it passes out of view, from the present into the past.

*You can't change the past. But you can make better choices in the future. Everything is interconnected. And pay more attention to your relationships. Be gentle with everyone, as I am gentle with you.*

"Gentle? What's gentle about all this?"

*You prayed for something for which being here is the answer. And now the man who fell from the sky is not the same who flew into it.*

I looked up into the stone-gray sky and out across the seemingly dead and abandoned city. I looked back to the egg and reaching up, placed my hand upon it. And for the second time I said out loud, "I think I can live with this now."

Chapter Three:

# Back by Popular Demand

With that, I returned, with no lucidity or memory of this event for about a week. As the fog of week-long anesthesia and coma-inducing drugs lifted, I came to realize that I was in a rehabilitation hospital. A familiar photo from my past was taped on the wall, the first photo my wife ever saw of me.

*With the Northern Alliance in northern Afghanistan, October, 2001*

It made sense she taped it there, to remind me of the man she fell in love with and wanted returned to her. She wanted to encourage me to heal back to that person, the best version of myself, as she saw it.

I've touched on my past life, before my NDE and visiting the In Between. As someone who was used to taking big chances with my life, it's no surprise the things I attempted and pulled off.

Even my near-death experience is more unique than 99.9% of those reported. No tunnels. No dead loved ones. No Jesus. No life review. No boundary of no return. Before my NDE, my ego was pretty wrapped up in being that person in the photograph. This was how I defined myself. I was interested in spiritual things and by comparison I could honestly say I tried to live as a spiritual person. But now, post-NDE, I looked at that photo and knew I wasn't *him* anymore. That person died in the crash. I looked down at my beaten up body and saw that as what I would be building new upon now. I knew the man in the photo, but now I was someone else. Something else. And the best guess I had as to who that might be was deep in the depersonalized new best-version of myself I met in the In Between, someone who had no memory or attachment to anyone or anything here on this planet. And there was no going back from that. I guess that you could say that what I thought I knew before was based on intellectual learning. Now it was woven into fabric of my being. Welcome to Jim 2.0. Now I just needed to get to know him.

*Jim Bruton, with NBC News in Iraq, 2003*

My recognizable face was that of an NBC News war journalist and if you're thinking I'm one of those people who isn't content to live a normal life, that is true. I've always needed to push against something, to have a challenge and I've always loved risk.

That risk now took the form of an erector set encasing my right leg. Weaving in and out of my leg were many metal rods I later learned formed an "Ex-Fit". I could not move that leg, so I just looked at it- swollen and resting, raised on a couple of pillows. It was a little painful, but mostly from the way I felt the metal rods twisting my leg. I shared the sensation with the nurse and she pointed out that the rods were bending my leg into all the right orientations for proper healing.

While we were talking, my nurse, Jenn, looked closely at my chin. She commented on how good it looked and handed me a mirror. My chin looked normal. I asked what she meant. She described the injury of my chin being shredded from my plane crash. I couldn't imagine what type of cosmetic surgeon they found, but it was great work. I could see three fine lines like natural age-creases going down my chin but based on them and how my chin moved when I spoke, no one would ever know I had an injury. Simply amazing work.

My doctor came in and together, he and Jenn explained the rest of my injuries. All in all, I felt fine but knew my recovery would take time. We reviewed a daily schedule for physical and occupational therapy and approved it.

I liked all of my hospital staff and doctors. I felt attended to and shared my appreciation. Honestly, I felt pretty good about the situation.

With each passing day, the effects of the anesthesia, physical shock and pain killers lessened, and I began to think more normally and remember things.

I thought of my work. As a contractor, if I didn't work, I didn't get paid. By the grace of God one of my earlier employers had contacted me a few months prior regarding an investment they had made on my behalf. They asked whether I wanted to reinvest it or cash it in. I thought about it the entire summer, then decided to cash it in. I received the check on October 1$^{st}$, paid my taxes on October 3$^{rd}$ and crashed on October 6$^{th}$, now with enough money to support us for those three months with the taxes taken care of. Talk about a synchronicity.

I had planned on spending the remaining funds toward a vacation in the UK for Dana and me. We had planned to leave the day after I crashed, so this changed everything. After a few weeks in the hospital, I thought if everything had gone according to plan, we would have already returned and gotten back into the normal swing of things. Instead, here I was. I told my nurse, "this may not be the vacation I wanted, but it might be the one I needed." All in all, I would be "on vacation" for three months before going back to work, and that included the end-of-year and New Year holidays.

The memory of the In Between started to descend upon me in full. The egg, the gears, the gothic experience in its entirety. It's as if every time I played it over in my head, more detail would come. My wife brought my laptop from home and brought me a newspaper clipping reporting my crash.

*Report of my crash in the local Republican American newspaper*

I smiled, thinking this was some great press in general. The articles quoted it all: my invention that reduced a satellite TV truck into a backpack had changed how breaking news could be transmitted live by video from the most remote, extreme and harsh locations previously impossible; the tracking system with an accuracy of less than 1-degree over 22,500 miles allowed you to roof mount the system and drive around with it, having an over-satellite videoconference with anyone; and my modified system that integrated wearable and swallow-able biometrics destined for the International Space Station, becoming a NASA Principal Investigator and Lecturer at Yale University School of Medicine. We tested this experiment two years in a row on Mount Everest. My work was written up in *The New York Times*, *WIRED* and some widely read trade magazines.

Again, I looked at the photo. I was no longer that person, but someone else.

This change was reflected when a friend asked me if I had a bad premonition on the day of my flight and following crash. I answered that there is always a sense of caution when test flying an experimental aircraft but now I felt guided to answer, "Beyond premonition, what if I had full knowledge of what was about to happen? Would I have had the guts to get into the cockpit anyway?" I believe this was the right answer, though I can't say I would have made it. If God wants to take you aside for some personal time, what price is too great to pay? Do you really think you can escape going?

Everyone who came into my room noticed the cigar photo with the Afghans. If they asked about it, and most did, the discussions would begin with the usual whiz-bang of living that kind of life, but for the more soulful people, the stories took on a deeper angle. Interestingly, when in the war zones, people could speak on a spiritual level. One time, after I was in a firefight in which we were grossly outnumbered, we called in a couple of Apache helicopters to drop two 5-story buildings into the dust using Hellfire missiles. The surprising thing was that at no time was I scared. When I caught up with my mentor, I asked about this. "Why wasn't I scared?" Actually, I felt a Zen-like peace that I would have only thought was a rumor. My mentor responded without pause, "I can tell you why. It's because that in that moment, everything was True." What do you do with that? It felt so *right*. And really, there was nothing more to add to it.

Many other spiritual discussions were enjoyed at night on the battlefield. I shared these with anyone visiting my room who seemed interested. Sharing more stories from the battlefield, I recounted how I told a few guys one night that "it's easy to find God, but it's hard to become a Man." Again, a statement that simply feels *right*.

I took it a little further, saying many are the people who "find God", but they don't do one more thing about it after that. I would further suggest some or many people didn't even "find" God but of course that's a judgment I can't make. But to be a Man is a moment by moment decision. Man is a noble creature when he listens to his higher voice. This state of nobility I believe to be our natural state. But because the siren songs of this world call us to vice over virtue, the higher callings are drowned out. And if you fill up your heart with all the things and desires for this world, then where have you left room for God?

As my attachments to things past felt so apparently different by the changing sense of self caused by my NDE, I began typing up my experience, fearing it would fade. How was I to know it never would? While confusing at first, I knew my experience of the In Between was significant; it didn't feel like a memory as much as it did an actual experience, and one that was somehow still occurring. With each iteration in my memory, details added layers of depth to the experience, and the sheer *oomph* hit harder. The In Between wasn't a place you go to or come from, it's simply a place you *are*. A few days later, I shared my odd thought and memory of the In Between with Jenn, my morning shift nurse.

She was definitely the A-Team and proactive in my care. Jenn thought of everything, was light of spirit and buoyant in every way. I'd begun to notice that she liked to simply hang out, so we talked about many things and life in general. I think it was the timing of when she came in one morning and where I was in my head with the In Between. I asked her if she would mind me sharing with her a really odd thought, something I'd been wrestling with. She indicated interest and leaned against the wall. This was the first time I'd shared my NDE and the In Between. I had no idea what to expect, but I felt more compelled to talk about it than afraid of what Jenn or anyone else might think.

I told her what I could remember and said how more and more of it was coming back every moment. I wondered if I had died and if this time in the hospital was nothing more than a mental construct I created to come to grips with the fact I was dead, and soon the other shoe would drop.

I wasn't expecting her to cry. That surprised me. I asked if her being a nurse in a hospital, seeing people die at a higher frequency than most of us, was the reason she was so distressed with the idea of it happening to me.

"Because you're magical", she answered. I gave her my best INFJ (Introversion (I), Intuition (N), Feeling (F), Judgment (J)) stare and asked her what she meant. Jenn explained that in her entire medical career, she had never seen anyone get so much personal attention from so many doctors. One even wanted to start a business with me and I would join international conference calls while doped up on strong pain killers, flat on my back with my caged leg up in the air. While every patient had one doctor's visit for fifteen minutes per day, I had three to five in there at any given time, spending up to an hour just talking about life. It was something she'd never before seen.

Over the next few weeks, more and more of the In Between came to me and filled in the blanks. I felt compelled to talk about it with more people. If I were to be left with a stranger for more than five minutes, guess what I would start talking about? I just couldn't help myself.

Every day one sense of self emerged further from the fog while another one receded into it. As the depersonalized, conscious being from the In Between entered the room, the man in the photo on the wall stepped back. There was no room for them both. To my wife, the photo was the best version of myself- my match.com photo. My dawning awareness was that my best version wasn't this but who I was, who I am, in the In Between, stripped of everything. Knowing not the oscillating sine wave of joy and sorrow, but the main axis of acquiescence, flowing in the Impossible Now beyond time, in a continual state of Letting Go.

*Clackety-clack* went the gears as one choice changed a million billion next choices.

One day when I was feeling that connection to the In Between, I sensed a conversation with God. In this new conversation, He removed from me the representation of alcohol and asked what I wanted to do with it. If I wanted to take it into my future, He would carry it for me. If I wanted to leave it behind, He would remove all attachment to it. It would be as if I'd never had a drink and it would have no pull on me. Let me say here that I am not an alcoholic. I would have a drink or two when I returned home from a stressful day and my wife was concerned about it. Anyway, I said, "Leave it behind". He said, "Alright" and away it went. I've not had a drink since and am not inclined to. I've been a vegetarian since I was 20 and just like eating meat is something other people do, so is drinking alcohol. This drove home the lesson the power of Letting Go. I also wondered if this was an example of how the latent created the manifest. That if drinking alcohol was a gear I'd thrown out but this "conversation with God" was how I would re-interpret and manifest that sublime action.

*Clackety-clack.*

Time passed and I became a little stronger for increasing amounts of physical therapy. I got to where I could stand for 30 seconds, then 60, then 90 and eventually I was using a walker to walk down the hall, before running out of breath. It's amazing, how something we take for granted like walking, can be a feat when you're weak. When my therapists thought I was strong enough, they rolled me in a wheelchair down to the PT room- where there were more things for us to use, pads, parallel bars to walk between, etc. But when they rolled me up to the doorway, I shot out both hands and took hold of the door frame and simply said, "No".

Fortunately for me, they simply said, "OK, we have a private room over here we can use" and so we went in there. I have no idea why I couldn't go into that room full of people but it was if I'd hit a wall. I've thought of every reason I can imagine but none apply. I wasn't embarrassed, fearful, or anything. I just knew I wasn't going in there. I'm sure it was something my empathy was picking up on but not translating to my conscious mind.

*Clackety-clack.*

Seven weeks after my crash, I went home. It was a complication several days before my planned discharge that had me go home a day early. When speaking to my friendly group of five doctors, they noticed I was short of breath while talking, even though I was sitting.

My main doctor, Dr. Singh, had a hunch and ordered an MRI scan. His hunch was correct, I had almost two liters of fluid around my left lung, a lingering result of the damage sustained in my crash. I was rushed back to Hartford Hospital where they drained it. By now, I was really tired of being in the hospital and when it was determined that I could go straight home from there, we fled. I had a coarse shawl around me and was wearing my skimpy hospital clothes and she was running to the car, pushing my wheelchair through the front doors and down the sidewalk. We were laughing and I kept looking over my shoulder as if we were about to be caught and dragged back inside. You would have thought we robbed a bank or were refugees escaping from a tyrant. I didn't know how much I loved freedom until then. We called the rehab hospital and they packed up my things in readiness for us to drop by. We retrieved my few things at the rehab hospital then stopped by a medical equipment store and picked up my wheelchair, shower bench, walker and crutches. Then we drove home. Dana kept turning around while driving to take me in, making me feel like I was a Christmas present. It was pure and beautiful and honest. I knew I was loved.

I slept on a pullout sofa on the ground floor and rolled around in a wheelchair most of the time, practicing the use of my crutches. To go upstairs for a shower on my shower bench, I butt-hopped up and down the stairs, still keeping weight off my right leg. It felt so good to take a proper shower.

My cousin John came over to visit and built me a ramp in the garage that I used to wheel myself into the house with my wheelchair. It's still there! When you have something built so well and out of love, well, you don't just get rid of it the first chance you get. My family bent over backwards to help me. My youngest daughter had just gotten her Driver's License and was happy to drive me back and forth to my doctors' appointments and I think the doctors enjoyed talking to her more than they did me. I never heard even a sigh of complaint from my family. Our housekeeper and her husband, from Brazil, made me some vegetarian Portuguese dishes and brought them to my bedside. Our dentist and her husband, who was my flight medical doctor, extended themselves to help with the medical questions and needs. I am still touched by the kindness from our family and friends.

As I settled into life again, I noticed changes on all fronts. Physically, other than the obvious work with physical therapy, I noticed that my sense of taste had lessened, so I picked snacks for their sweet or savory sensation rather than their flavor. My sense of smell seemed more sensitive- and I avoided standing near people with perfume or cologne. My vision changed too- improving to 20/15, yet now I needed glasses because things seemed to ebb and flow in and out of focus, somewhat like the way I saw things in the In Between. I also didn't need sunglasses anymore, unless the low angle of the sun in winter made the light come directly into my eyes.

I noticed how I couldn't "multitask", or work in a distracted manner. If I was writing a check for my daughter, she couldn't talk to me at the same time. I went to a Yale neurologist and she tested me for several hours. Her results said that I was impaired for memory and attention. Oddly, the results also said that in struggling to solve a problem, I did better when struggling alone than when given a hint. This told me that having been Present in the In Between had left its indelible stamp on me; when I focus on one thing, it is like a laser. During that time, nothing else exists. That's my attention "deficit;" when I focused on one thing, I can't remember what I just said or remember where I was going. That's my memory "deficit".

I kept writing of my experience in the In Between, I was now calling it the IB, and spoke about my re-entry. I test flew my story with a few people who I considered trustworthy. By that I mean self-introspective people would read without initial judgment and with an open mind. Of this small population, some responded with enthusiasm and wanted to hear more.

I reach out to Tim Pitts, a friend who has a Rolodex from God and he sent me back a 25-page template of questions about me and my story to fill out. He sent it to his brother in law who is head of marketing for Double Day publishing and he said that while he was drawn into my story right away, I needed to go make friends with someone who with a professional writing background unless I wanted to spend years developing one. Tim reached out to ten professional writers- six men and four women.

All the men said they were too busy. All the women couldn't get enough of it and I spoke to them all. One was a teacher at Princeton and we hit it off - but she was busy and headed to England to do Shakespeare theater that summer at the Globe and we couldn't synch our times; she would have been perfect. Then there was another woman who the next weekend got arrested for drunk driving, handed my project to a male friend, who was too busy, and his writer-girlfriend visited him, saw it, took it on and that was Julia, the one I did work with.

*Clackety-clack.*

A couple of prospective writers asked, "What the hell is this all about?" which I thought funny and endearing. The only ones whose responses puzzled me were those who went silent and I've never heard from again. I'm curious but not saddened. We weren't close but at least in one or two cases these people drove some distance to visit me when I returned home. Now, silence. If my story hit them in a certain way to cause this, I'm curious how. Perhaps they didn't like it, were ambivalent, or liked it but simply had no words or response. I felt that I was more present there than here, saying one day, "The In Between isn't a place you go to or come from. It's simply a place you are."

One morning I came down to get my coffee, and noticed our parrot outside his cage, playfully hanging on the bottom of his open door. My wife had uncovered him from his night's sleep. But when I microwaved my coffee and was walking to my office, I realized that his cage was locked, and he was inside it. A few days earlier, I heard some friends argue at a get-together and later, when I mentioned it to my next-door neighbor, he had no memory at all of it. Another curious new phenomenon appeared as well; when someone popped into my head, he or she then contacted me within three days no matter how far away in distance or time since we'd last seen each other. One person was from 35 years ago. I began watching my mind more to understand the changes.

I mentioned this to my wife one day. She said something odd. "Perhaps the edges of your reality are fraying". I thought about that and said nothing. Later, when I asked her, she didn't remember saying it.

Over the next few weeks, more "fraying at the edges" of my reality continued. I began lucid dreaming, where I could choose to fly, or not, at will. I began to realize that this was a power to be used wisely, not just for the jubilant freedom from gravity. I started to combine it with things I read in spiritual books, and that formed the reality of the dreams. In one dream I finished upon waking, I saw myself on a beach at dawn and a decrepit figure in a shawl on the other side of a fence, holding a horse by the reins. Within my head, I heard a celestial gentle but high-pitched sound and with a gentle force of will, slowly levitated up and over the fence to stand beside him. As I did so, I listened more intently to the Sound and felt waves of compassion for this wretched creature, which now I knew represented some sad condition of the human spirit. I sensed the difference between the actor and role they were damned to play. As I landed, we both looked into each other's eyes and whatever he thought of the situation, he surrendered his horse's reins to me and walked away.

Then I awoke.

Even at this time, I still wasn't sure what type of experience I had. I began to research the "cosmic" egg, the choices that setup our destinies, the gothic otherworldly landscape and so on. For a time, I wondered if I'd gone to Purgatory.

One day as I sat there researching, I got bored and decided to select an On-Demand movie on television. I looked at the trailers of several then saw one that visually clicked 100% with what I was researching. I paid for the movie and watched it, waiting for the scene that caught my attention. It literally was in the last scene and I mean fifteen seconds before the movie ended and the credits rolled. But it was worth waiting for. Even now, it is the inspiration for the In Between graphic I use in this book and in my talks. I added the egg, sculpted with a laser and the clouds from a news photo taken of Manhattan in the summer of 2018 when tornadoes were reported in the areas nearby.

Once I composited the image with the above elements, the destroyed city, the storm clouds and the laser carved egg, I knew I had captured what the IB looked like during my time there. This helped anchor me somewhat. I loved the imminent explosion the image looked capable of; I was trying to convey the emotion of raw terror if you were suddenly standing before the largest tornado-causing storm in human history, bearing down on you and you've no place to hide- the fear forcing you to flee or fight and then the realization that anything other than surrender is useless. When you realize you can't outrun death, you might as well turn around and look it in the eye.

Re-energized, I felt this continual push from the In Between to keep writing, keep remembering, keep pushing in. I began to realize this was a Near-Death Experience and I directed my reading there, downloading audio books on the subject.

I discovered IANDS and NDERF, two major NDE organizations where thousands of experiencers post their reports, discuss all aspects of NDEs and announce national and local meetings. I found the stories of NDEs interesting but not finding anything similar to mine, soon dug into the pages discussing the patterns and common challenges which often follow this transcendental experience, ranging from initial reactions from friends and family to relationship challenges, the after-effects of the experience and how to integrate the profound with the mundane. I found podcasts and YouTube videos.. In gathering more details of the key attributes of an NDE, I was coming to see how unique my one in a million experience was, within an already one in a million population.

On the IANDS (International Association for Near-Death Studies) website, it has this list of characteristics common in a majority of NDEs:

- Intense emotions: commonly of profound peace, well-being, love; others marked by fear, horror, loss
- A perception of seeing one's body from above (called an out-of-body experience, or OBE), sometimes watching medical resuscitation efforts or moving instantaneously to other places
- Rapid movement through darkness, often toward an indescribable light

- A sense of being "somewhere else," in a landscape that may seem like a spiritual realm or world
- Incredibly rapid, sharp thinking and observations
- Encounter with deceased loved ones, possibly sacred figures (the Judges, Jesus, a Saint) or unrecognized beings, with whom communication is mind-to-mind; these figures may seem consoling, loving, or terrifying
- A life review, reliving actions and feeling their emotional impact on others
- In some cases, a flood of knowledge about life and the nature of the universe
- Sometimes a decision to return to the body

P.M.H. Atwater, one of the most prolific NDE researchers, adds a few other attributes to the IANDS website:

- Passing through a dark tunnel. Or black hole or encountering some kind of darkness. This is often accompanied by a feeling or sensation of movement or acceleration. "Wind" may be heard or felt.
- Ascending toward a light at the end of the darkness. A light of incredible brilliance, with the possibility of seeing people, animals, plants, lush outdoors, and even cities within the light.
- Greeted by friendly voices, people or beings who may be strangers, loved ones, or religious figures. Conversation can ensue, information or a message may be given.
- Seeing a panoramic review of the life just lived, from birth to death or in reverse order, sometimes becoming a reliving of the life rather than a dispassionate viewing. The person's life can be reviewed in its entirety or in segments. This is usually accompanied by a feeling or need to assess loss or gains during the life to determine what was learned or not

learned. Other beings can take part in this judgment like process or offer advice.

- A reluctance to return to the earth plane, but invariably realizing either their job on earth is not finished or a mission must yet be accomplished before they can return to stay.
- Warped sense of time and space. Discovering time and space do not exist, losing the need to recognize measurements of life either as valid or necessary.
- Disappointment at being revived. Often feeling a need to shrink or somehow squeeze to fit back in to the physical body. There can be unpleasantness, even anger or tears at the realization they are now back in their bodies and no longer on "The Other Side."

I experienced some of these attributes but not all, and those I did were significant.

*Visiting with P.M.H. Atwater in her home in early 2019*

The key features missing from my NDE were:

- **Tunnel.** I did not see or travel through a tunnel. I simply appeared in the In Between. And when I left, I remember having an awareness that I was leaving and a feeling more than a perception of leaving It, but I have no memory of exactly how I left, possibly because of the indefinite threshold between a non-physical super conscious state and the anesthetized and physically impaired body I returned to. Because of the quantum nature of the experience is full of super-positioned probabilities where time doesn't exist, it follows there is an uncertainty of boundaries and edges, where something is and where it is not. Therefore the threshold between the non-physical and the physical can even be indefinite, and for those having transcendent or shamanistic experiences, this is commonly reported.

  The super-conscious state is defined by its presence in the single moment, called the Impossible Now by the In Between. It is here I was depersonalized down to zero -- no memory, no emotion, no attachment, no fear or desire- just conscious and aware only of my mission -- to remove those gears representing unfortunate choices in my future, would-be obstacles to my spiritual journey.

- **Meeting of Loved Ones**. I didn't see anyone else. But I wasn't alone, the disembodied voice made that apparent. I believe this and the dead landscape around me provided an environment for me to focus without the distractions of anyone to which I had an attachment. In a dead city, there is little of interest to explore. In a solitary world, there is no one to talk to other than the world itself.

- **Unconditional love**. There were no hugs or warm, loving feelings. But in a military boot camp, there is no feeling of love from your drill instructor either. Its design and purpose are to help you survive what comes next, to strengthen your ability to stay on task and to create not courage, but Heart. That and to make better informed decisions to ensure your survival and success. This is where love may be latent in design but not manifest in action. At home, love is about hugs. In boot camp, it is about getting your butt kicked. Two sides of the same coin, both sets of circumstances are meant to help you get to whatever the next stage is.

- **Boundary of No Return**. None detected. It would have served little purpose anyway. If someone had said, "if you stay any longer you can't go back", I would have asked "go back where?" If they had responded, "to your family" I would have answered, "what family?" That is how far gone, how depersonalized down to Zero, I was in the In Between.

Regarding the bullet above of intense emotion, another aspect commonly reported is Joy. I felt no emotion at all: joy, love, fear or sorrow. It was about Mission and Purpose, with an almost ruthless edge to it. I was more focused on the *process* of setting things up to be right than experiencing the *content* of "right living" at that time. After all, you can build a swimming pool without ever getting wet.

By design, I was put into this gray and colorless place to not be distracted; there was one thing and one thing only I could do. And the way in which I would do it was with nothing better than the pain of these possible but tempting choices while still in their probably states. That was more humbling than I have words to express. I have thought about this and see the wisdom of not allowing me to see the choices I was discarding. What if I saw myself winning the lottery but becoming the biggest jerk who ever lived? Of course, if most of us could see that possibility in our future, we would beg God to let us be wealthy and we would promise to not be mean to people afterward. But God mercifully removed the temptation of seeing what was being discarded, and let pain be the guide. For in the end, after a pleasant turned bad decision is made and fulfilled, pain is all that is left.

I was told the Who, what, when and where of the discarded choice were of less importance than seeing and understanding the beauty of things fit and refit together. How everything was inter-connected. The interconnectivity reinforced a natural tendency for me to be less distracted by content and more intent on process. I was there to learn the formulas of the universe rather than plug in values and practice graphing their outcomes. Using pain to select the futures helped reduce attachment to actions or their outcomes, which leads to a later thought or two on the creation of karma.

This is what an analysis of my spiritually transformative expe-rience gave me. While it sinks in, let's go back to my childhood and look for clues that brought me to my NDE; how perfectly teed-up the experience was based on the questions I asked with the way I lived my life.

Part III:

# Dawning Awareness

Chapter Four:

# Integration & Coping

*Here, we see life through the filters we want.*
*There, we see life through the filters we need.*

Everyone who reports back their Near-Death Experience says how tailor-made, how individualized it was, right down to the most secret and subtle of things. Things which consciously seemed chaotic or in no apparent order all now appear to be part of a larger, organized pattern.

I wonder if it's the same experience but tailor- based on who we are at the time and what we need. If we looked at the outer life of someone, would an NDE appear to be a huge, unexpected quantum jump from their inner life, or the next, most natural next step in their evolution?. If they haven't done anything "good" or "bad" to find themselves in the outer circumstances the world calls a predicament, then the jump isn't so much the result of a pull from having done something right or wrong as it is a push to get them to where they need to be.

One realization I've had after my NDE is how powerful thoughts are. With the inability to work distractedly as I did before ("multi-tasking"), I find this single-mindedness of attention is a hindrance sometimes, but generally an advantage. My thoughts bear more fruit in the outer world even when I don't appear to be directly involved. This is also part of being more present.

I naturally became who I am there; every day I was drawn more and more into being that person. If I didn't seem to be that, believe me, it was because I was trying to be like everyone else "here", to just get along. My failure was evident in my separation from my wife. Yet my superpower, empathy with everyone else, amazes. My daughter, who is a straight-A student in university, says I think in 4-D.

With that, I've looked through my own life for clues. Were there moments all throughout my life that, like pearls strung together, brought me to this transcendental experience?

First, my life is certainly one of many realized childhood dreams. When I was little, I would watch *Wild Kingdom*, followed by *The Wonderful World of Disney* every Sunday evening. I remember watching Marlin Perkins and Jim Fowler travel the world, helping wild animals and having one adventure after another. One night, as I watched our small black and white television on the kitchen table, I asked, "what does it take to do that for a living?"

During the day, I would read through *Popular Mechanics* magazines when they talked about how life would be so much more relaxed when we would rocket pack to work and then wind down with tourism to the moon by the year 2000. I wanted to live in that future *right now* and would draw up one invention after another to help usher in such a future. A few years later, my father became a professional pilot and would fly with my mother and me around northern Florida for fun. When a movie came to the cinema about flying, we would go to see, most notably, *Those Magnificent Men in Their Flying Machines* and *The Blue Max*. I really liked aviation during its age of discovery and when aircraft were put together with wood, fabric, brass, copper and wire, they were beautiful in their primitive nature and a wonder of creation.

Who knew these things that excited me, as doodles in the margins of my notebook paper called distractions by my teachers, would sprout into significant contributions of my being here, on earth, themselves an expression of who I am? Who thought like that in the 1960s?

As the years passed, I put my dreams in a drawer and got on with the business of growing up. My parents were busy with their grown-up lives, so there wasn't much encouragement in my dreaming of animals on the other side of the planet, science fiction books with titles like *The Infinite Worlds of Maybe* or building airplanes the hard way. My parents talked more about the need to study hard and make more realistic choices that ensure an easier road than they had traveled.

Yet now I look at how those dreams became real with only the power of my imagination and insatiable curiosity.

As I sit typing this, I look at some of the many photos that hang on the wall, capturing years of having lived and worked in Africa. Collectively, they are represented in a corner across the room by my Emmy for work on a National Geographic television special. Bringing it back full circle to *Wild Kingdom,* I became friends with co-host Jim Fowler and hosted his first online chat session. While at the helm of *Old World Safaris,* the tour company I founded with my first wife, I was asked by Burt Avedon, who owned Willis & Geiger Outfitters, to design a safari camera jacket based on my work in the field. In the catalogue it was titled the *Willis & Geiger Skeleton Coast Camera Jacket.* Side note: Willis & Geiger Outfitters was an expeditionary outfitting company in the United States, outfitting Teddy Roosevelt, Roald Amundsen, Charles Lindbergh, Amelia Earhart, Sir Edmund Hillary and the Flying Tigers. Pretty much, wherever legends were made in the 20th Century, they were there.

*Breakfast at camp in Namibia, Cover shot of our film for National Geographic Television, Willis & Geiger Skeleton Coast jacket I designed.*

Vintage aircraft memorabilia decorate another wall in my home, including photos from the two historical reproduction aircraft I built and flew: the 1917 Fokker DR-1(Triplane) and the 1933 French Flying Flea. Both fascinations from my childhood, I read all I could about them, drew picture after picture working out the details of their construction and built models of the Fokker, as none existed of the Flea. The Fokker was my boyhood preoccupation with the aerial warfare of WW1 and the aircraft I built was a faithful reproduction the Red Baron's, though the black and white striped paint scheme was my own. The Flying Flea was a more whimsical design but one I loved and fantasized about flying when I was a child; it looked like it came from the same set of movie props as *Chitty Chitty Bang Bang*.

*Here I am with my childhood's favorite historical aircraft-*
*1917 Fokker Triplane, N41 Airfield, Waterbury, CT*

*1933 Flying Flea, N41 Airfield, Waterbury, CT*

As to the science fantasy future and how that desire manifested into my life, as with many boys growing up in the 1960s, our fantasies were driven by constant advances in the NASA space program and fueled monthly with the pages of *Popular Mechanics* promising flying saucers in every garage, something the magazine is still teased about. I wanted to be an astronaut and I wanted to invent something cool and futuristic. In the 4th Grade, something clicked inside me and I began to draw inventions as fast as I could conceive them. Granted, these were the types of drawings you'd expect from a 10-year-old with an imagination. In the 7th Grade, we drove from Jacksonville to visit Cape Kennedy and I loved feeling closer to my dream of spaceflight. Mom took my picture standing at the top of the ladder by the entry door of a reproduction of the Lunar Excursion Module, which the astronauts used to land on the Moon. My dream of touching space in one way or another and inventing something futuristic came when I figured out how to shrink a satellite-television truck into a backpack and transmit live video from all seven continents as well as underwater from the Titanic, both Polar Regions, Mt. Everest and several warzones.

1967 was an interesting year. My father flew a small Cessna with my mother and me all the way from Florida to California. We went to Disneyland and as you would expect, the park itself was amazing for a budding 6th grader visiting for the first time. After faithfully watching the Sunday night television show "The Wonderful World of Disney", all the movies, reading the picture books and listening to the songs, this made it all real. For many children, this may be one of the first real validations of their dreams and fantasies. It's easy to see why grownups enjoy it as much as kids. One is seeing it for the first mind-blowing time, the other is revisiting unfinished business in their childhood.

As you can imagine, in how much I loved science fiction and the optimistic visions of the future, the House of the Future was the absolute manifestation of all that potential. Of all the cool gadgets in the home to capture my imagination, I was drawn to the videophone, with its streamlined design and white Lexan plastic housing. I remember thinking how cool it would be to have that one day in my home!

*Monsanto's House of the Future*
*& Video Phone, Disneyland,*
*1967, Anaheim, California*

Fast forward to 1993, on the coast of Namibia in southwestern Africa and pause for a moment. Twenty-six years after I visited Disneyland, Disney sent a film crew to the other side of the world, to a place that translates as "The Big Nothing" (Namibia) then finds me in the middle of nowhere and relights the torch originally lit in this weird, impossible memory that united my love for wanting to live in a futuristic world and create sci-fi inventions. And now, with a strong media background under my belt and the credibility my ideas would bring, I could do it.

I flew back to the USA to meet with the manufacturer of the satphone and tell them that I wanted to be able to transmit live video into the World Wide Web (created only that year, 1993), for people to see in real time the beauty of the natural world. Then I went to talk to Bell Labs about sponsorship, and they liked the idea too. It would be several years before the digital satellites would launch that would support my original vision, but when it came time, *yes*, I was the first in the world to do it.

Here is the range of development, in 3 photos:

*The satellite telephone like Disney used, Namibia, 1993*

*My first public transmission, Mexico, October 31, 1996*

**Technology** | CYBERTIMES          The New York Times ON THE WEB

| Home | Site Index | Site Search | Forums | Archives | Marketplace |

August 3, 1998

## Reporting Live, Indiana Jones-Style

By LISA NAPOLI

**W**hen documentary producer Jim Bruton first saw a satellite phone, it was 1993, he was in Africa, and a figurative light bulb went off above his head.

"I thought, 'Man, I've got to have one of these,'" he said, imagining the communications possibilities from the far-flung places around the globe where he typically shot his nature films.

Tracking down a phone and dissecting it was just the beginning of what has become a digital-age Indiana Jones-like quest. Bruton -- who possesses the bearing and the rugged looks of an explorer straight from central casting -- has invented a television field production package that puts the transmission technology currently available in a giant, half-million dollar satellite truck into a backpack. He claims his rig makes broadcasting live pictures from anywhere in the world possible -- with just ten minutes of setup time -- calling it a "TV truck in a suitcase."

Thomas Mcdonald for CyberTimes

Jim Bruton demonstrating the satellite equipment that allows him to send television images from almost anywhere in the world.

Bruton has experimented with his system in a variety of places you'd expect to find a member of the Explorers Club. In May, he set up in base camp at Mount Everest, beaming back information for a Yale telemedicine project to monitor the physiology of climbers, as well as broadcasting live video for segments on the major networks. For CNN earlier this year, he transmitted live video from the Persian Gulf aboard the USS Independence. He has field-produced for Discovery Channel Online's coverage of the raising of the Titanic, and for the Web-based adventure magazine Mungo Park's "Journey of the Wise Men" -- a recreation of the biblical journey from Iran, through Syria and Jordan and finally to Israel.

*Story in the New York Times, August, 1998*

As the only person in the world for a time who could do this, my work expanded from world adventurer to NASA Principal Investigator and Lecturer at Yale University School of Medicine to NBC News war journalist.

There was another dream I had as a child; to know God. I don't have anything on the wall to show my accomplishments in this regard, but I have some things I've picked up along the way to prove my interest. I also have some stories of how I took a serious step or two closer to Him. Please remember these a few pages from now as they become more significant *after* my NDE.

As I've shared, 1967 was an unusual year for me. The two stories below occurred two years later, in 1969. But while the Disney experience took about twenty-five years to bear fruit, the ones below took almost fifty.

My school bus stopped at a simple, wooden ramshackle house to pick up a little boy and girl, a brother and sister. He was kind of a tough kid but quiet and he kept to himself. I think it was a defensive reflex to an entire bus of his peers stopping outside his humble home and being reminded of how poor he was.

His sister looked like she'd been in a car accident and gone through the windshield. Her entire face was scarred with the badly healed cuts that misshaped her face. One day the bus stopped and they got on board. Except for today Bonnie looked normal and had an outgoing personality. Same height, physical build, carriage, hairstyle, and color. Except she had absolutely no deformity and she was engaging. I know because she and I sat next to each other on that day. Now I know how unbelievable this is but I've learned since that when such things happen, we don't freak out, we go with it. So did I. On the way home that afternoon, we again sat next to each other and she chatted all the way home.

The next morning, she looked like her other self, got on the bus and I don't think even looked at me, but I can't remember; I am not sure if we ever talked again either. It was an experience that foreshadowed some interesting post-NDE phenomena.

About a month later, I was asking my parents about God and wearing them out with all the questions. They finally lost patience and told me to go down the road to church, Highlands Baptist Church, on Broward Road. The next Sunday morning, I put on my suit and walked past the few houses to the church, ready with all my questions.

I sat in the pew and saw the minister up on the stage, talking to a team of helpers and obviously too busy preparing his sermon to deal with me. Looking up at the clock counting down to the service, I oriented myself by watching him, his body language and demeanor, looking at the crowd around me and getting a general sense of what it was like to be in church.

My issue then, and now, with most sermons is that for a kid, "open your heart to Jesus" literally means nothing. Conceptually I had no idea what that meant or how to do it. To know you want God but to be given the way in gibberish caused only frustration. Add to that the impression it makes on a child to be called a sinner who will burn in Hell unless he unlocks the gibberish. The child starts to wonder if "their" heaven would his Hell. Imagine spending eternity with people like that. That would be one of my questions for the minister, for sure. If the instructions had been as they are for something like yoga and meditation, "sit in this position, breathe like this, relax, look into the darkness between your eyes, repeat this mantra....", reading like a checklist, well a child can follow that. Perhaps that's the problem with Christianity today; everyone is equally confused. How else are people unable to follow even the one, final commandment, to love your neighbor as yourself?

At the end of the service, I was ready to jump up and walk over to him but everyone in the church was suddenly in line ahead of me to shake his hand, invite him to lunch or dinner, gain some counsel or just get a blessing. If I thought he was too busy before his service, there was absolutely no chance of speaking to him now. I left and went home, determined to figure out a way to talk to him next week.

Next Sunday came and again I went to church. I thought to sit where I could get to the preacher at the end of his service more quickly and nearer the front of the long line of people.

But now we had a new preacher going through the same preparation as last week. I looked at a woman sitting next to me in the pew and asked where Reverend Coolidge was. She said primly, "we got rid of him." I asked why and she informed me that he did the unthinkable and married his daughter to a black man. To her, that explained everything, so I could now end the conversation and look straight ahead, which she would simply interpret as shock born of righteous indignation.

I was confused even worse than before. As I said, this was the South in the late 1960s, so it's not a guess as to what the predominant racial attitudes were and I was reminded of them right then. But it made no sense to me. Even then I knew that spirituality shouldn't care about such things, and yet here were such judgments flooding the church. I didn't even hear the sermon, and I couldn't leave before it ended as I realized I was stuck in the middle of the pew and if I tried to escape, all the crazy people might kill me. Best to lay low and run home at the first chance. Then I could ask my mom to help me sort it out. I never went back to that church.

My mother answered my questions as if she were remembering a bit of forgotten news. She confirmed that Reverend Coolidge had indeed married his daughter to a black man. Reverend Coolidge himself was a Cherokee Indian, a very interesting (I thought "cool") looking man. His younger daughter, Rita, was soaring in her music career and her slightly older sister, Priscilla, was also a rising star. Reverend Coolidge married Priscilla to Booker T (Jones), of Booker

T and the MGs, a legendary talent. It was natural that two such people might meet and fall in love, and I understood that. Yet the only thing so many people saw was color. Having been raised in this time and in this place, I also understood the prevailing sentiment of the congregation. But as a twelve-year-old in a racist, authoritarian culture, it mattered little what I thought. If I had voiced my displeasure, it would have ended with a heavy-duty spanking when I got home. In that there were no answers as to why it had to be that way, this is when I began to intuit the greater importance of understanding over answers. The ability to articulate it this succinctly wouldn't occur to me for almost a half-century.

Now, after my NDE, I understand God was saying it was wonderful I wanted to know Him. But if I walked the ways of man, I would come out with more questions than I went in with. If I walked with Him, He would tailor my lessons and where answers might fail, understanding would be given.

A simple indicator of this was driven home in my confusion understanding the sermons, which I've mentioned. "Open your heart", "Straighten up and fly right" and other colloquialisms are cute as a linguistic shorthand when you understand what they mean. Simply put, most things said in the church didn't provide me with actionable intelligence.

The congregation who had surely made sacrifices in their lives to know God as they could understand Him, who had made enemies and friends along that journey, were now kicking out their earthly shepherd for no worse a crime than he had dared marry his half-breed daughter to a black man. And *that* is apparently the lesson I went to church to learn, for it's the only one which presented itself. *That any honor man bestows, man can take away.*

For the rest of my spiritually-inclined childhood, I articulated my questions, gaining inspiration from books more with a covert spiritual theme than an obvious one, and mostly living an ethical life.

Not long after the Highlands Baptist Church debacle, we moved to Charlotte, NC. I made a high school friend in the apartment building where we lived who was open to some of my God talks. He told me of one teacher at our high school who was interested in similar things and had an after-class gathering of students who were like me, interested as well.

I didn't meet this teacher until two years later, in my senior year. He was a physics teacher and I went into his class remembering he might have enough experience to direct me to a line of inquiry or a path of yoga better suited to answer my questions. I can't remember what took me up to his desk one day, but somehow, I worked it in that I heard this sound since birth. His eyes lit up and he opened his drawer, pulled out a few printed sheets of suggested readings from his after-class get-together and invited me to join the group.

I went but we met infrequently, maybe three or four times. We were given excerpts from books by the great thinkers, beginning with Socrates. Interestingly, nothing here was religious but all of it was definitely philosophical. In a historic context, there were definitely some Big Questions intertwined about God, but as the suggested readings and therefore our discussions were across many ancient cultures, their various religions were more reference points in which to better understand the times and culture of these original discussions and discourses.

I found other opportunities to talk to the teacher about my own big questions and after a long time, he told me that he followed an Eastern path. Interestingly, the Sound that permeates all the universes is a key feature of this path, with the idea that through meditation, you can catch it and rise to higher planes and ultimately be free of this place. I received a new, more focused, reading list and began soaking up the wisdom of some of the previous teachers on this path. The goal here, as in the after-school meetings, was to appreciate how cultures the world over and throughout time were all asking the same important questions, so the emergent understanding was one of what we as human beings share, not how we differ.

We fell out of touch for about a year as I went off to my first year of college. In the spring of the following year, I called him up and we went out for pizza. Every time we would get together, he would give me another book.

My most prized book was the previously mentioned *The Book of Mirdad*, by Mikhail Naimy. Have you ever seen a work of art or read something so inspired that it stood out from everything else the artist or writer created? Just as Pachelbel's Canon remains a wedding favorite in its timeless beauty, so is *The Book of Mirdad*. When I researched Pachelbel, it looks like he built quite a career with one piece of music, which helped him become Court Composer. The piece was written in 1692. However, in listening to his other works, they are competently put together but none come close to his Canon. I feel like it was his one inspired piece. From what I understand of Mikhail Naimy, it's the same thing. I don't believe he wrote another book written as impactful as Mirdad. Interestingly, Naimy and Khalil Gibran were friends and writing associates.

Over time, no matter my inspiration of the week, it was becoming clear that having a teacher, or guru, would accelerate the journey I was on. But I couldn't find a living guru right there and then.

A few years later, I became so impatient I wrote asking for Initiation from one of the "competing" masters. A lady in our spiritual-social circle also was going to get Initiation and be put on the Path. We received letters of acceptance from this guru and were told where to go and when to be initiated. A few weeks before we were to go, I had a vision within my sleep. I saw myself walking down a long flight of stairs, deep into the earth. The walls and ceiling were close, providing only a narrow passage. I felt that everything was made of metal and painted navy gray. It was dimly lit but I kept walking.

I reached the bottom and walked into a room. There stood a robed figure with a few differently colored orbs of light floating in front of him. I couldn't see his face and intrigued by the orbs I didn't care. He said, "choose one", so I looked at them all, and finally did. I went up to it and showed my acceptance by putting my hands up near it, as if I were holding it. The robed figure said, "alright" and left back up the stairs, with a companion following.

I "held" my ball of light; it was purple in color. I stared at it and then into it. I felt drawn to it. I felt my attention pouring into it and picking up speed. I felt it going terribly fast and I started to panic; I felt like I was getting sucked into a black hole. I broke away from the orb and ran back to the stairs crying out, "no! This isn't what I want!" and everything went black. Never had a dream been so terrifying as this, either before or since. I'm not sure what time it was but probably around 2:00am or 3:00am in the morning. I turned on the light in my bedroom and didn't sleep the rest of the night. I picked up one of my teacher's books and began reading it and considering the vision I had to be a sign to not be initiated by this particular guru. The next day I wrote a letter saying, "no thanks" and was careful in sharing the details with my social group and the woman in particular who was happily awaiting initiation. I thought about the many ways I was warned and she was not. This could have meant the man was worse than a charlatan, with ability to do real evil, or he was simply not right for me, but maybe okay for her. She had received no warning and God or the True Master could have easily warned her as He did me.

About a month later, between 3:00 am and 3:30 am, I had another vision. I saw myself at night in a gray, old-fashioned town. I was on the sidewalk in front of a vintage movie theater. I stood there under the marquis in front of the ticket window when a young woman with dark hair suddenly rushed up to the window, breathless, and threw money down to purchase a ticket.

She ran inside, past the concessions, to where you actually walk into the dark theater. This "light break" area was comprised of a door frame in the wall of the lobby and one as the entrance to the theater. Between the two was a passage, a short hallway, if you will, with a lot of strands of heavy canvas like material hanging from the ceiling. The idea was that the strands made for easy passage back and forth as you brush past them. After the movie begins and everyone is seated, the strands are undisturbed and effectively blocking the light from the lobby.

As the lady was running toward this area, I was suddenly transported into the theater, waiting for her at the entryway. A black and white movie was playing and only a few people were seated. I heard the woman enter the hallway and she pushed through the strands of heavy material as if she didn't know they were there. Suddenly, I felt something inside my stomach like the slice of a sword with razor thinness; it felt cold and terrible. Out from within the strands, rolling by my feet into the theater, was the woman's head.

I awoke and looked at the clock, hence my accuracy of the time. I remember thinking what an odd lucid dream and soon returned to sleep. The next morning was Sunday and I was able to sleep in. At some point I awoke and thought about the dream. Then I remembered, at the exact time I had the dream, the woman I knew was to be initiated. I felt the original warning that much more. I had honestly forgotten about the Initiation and when it was until then.

Interestingly, this woman who had become a new initiate immediately pulled up stakes, moving somewhere no one knew and we never heard from her again.

Not all gifts offered are good things, even if they look like it.

When we read "Test the Sprits, for even Satan can appear as an Angel of Light", it makes sense. But what is the test to put before these things? Making the sign of the cross would not have done it, even for an ardent believer.

I put any more thought of rushing the process on hold. When the right guru became available, I'd hear about it.

When I left for Africa a few years later, I remember the first year feeling removed from everyone. It took an average of six to eight weeks to get a response to a mailed letter; there was no internet at the time. In my second year living in Etosha, I was visiting one of the ranger's homes one night and his newly arrived girlfriend had her books on the bookshelf. Several caught my eye because they had pictures of a Sikh on them. It turned out there is a large following for Sant Mat in South Africa and these books were authored by a master in a different line than my teacher's but who shared the same guru as my teacher's.

I borrowed one of the books and read it. As I did so, I felt happy. I also had a few lucid dreams spiritual in nature. I felt I was being given a sign. But it wasn't strong enough for me to pursue Initiation, given the fright from before.

When my then-wife and I left Africa for our home back in NC, our Satsangi friend in Namibia, the one who had lent me the book by this Master, called while we were enroute to say a new Master had been identified and would sometime "soon" be giving Initiation. We got as much information as we could as quickly as possible in a pre-email world, and with our travel back and forth between our homes in NC, the UK and Africa, it was impossible to pick a target location and date. I joked and asked if they could authorize a "Pay to the Bearer on Demand One Initiation" so that we could "cash" it anywhere and I don't think I ever received a serious response- understandably.

Eventually we did work out a schedule and we were both initiated at a country home in the UK. On this path, a Master can authorize senior disciples to perform Initiation for Him. It was so in this case. Interestingly, the elderly woman who initiated us was a disciple of Sawan Singh. I had always felt the most special affinity for him when I read his books, to the point I wondered if I had been one of his disciples before his passing in 1948 and my birth much later. To me, this was a quiet blessing that showed me I was on the right track.

I can't say I have been an exemplary disciple on my Path, but it has certainly provided a firm footing on which to stand and then to walk.

*I have no idea where this light bindi came from. Note the
mystical items in the corner, from my travels.*

And it's fair to ask, "What is Truth?" When you have any experience that transmutes knowledge from the intellectual to experience; whether physical, mental or spiritual, you have discovered Truth. Once out of the body, if you have *seen* quantum mechanics at work, you don't have to understand it in terms of esoteric mathematics any more than a caveman has to show you the calculus he used in throwing a spear along its parabolic arc to hit the wooly mammoth exactly where needed in order to kill the beast and feed his tribe.

A prehistoric person with no written language could show **blind** scientists a beautiful sunset worthy of a painting, but little good would it do them, for they cannot see. Their science and math can calculate what the sunset is doing when the temperature decreases on their faces as the sun eases below the horizon but they can't see or describe it. The changing pastels on the clouds, the gradient of the sky's blue turning to black or the emergence of the night's first stars and planets. All the scientists can understand and share is the mathematics of the experience, not the experience itself. That is the difference between who I was and who I am. Still, the baby steps taken to get this far were necessary and interesting to consider in connecting the dots, between my life and the In Between. Here are a few more stories from my earlier life…

Three years before my father died from cancer, I had a vision of his death. I dreamt I was standing in a forest glade and there was something nearby like an Eastern Indian interpretation of a gazebo. A friend of mine was sitting within the structure studying Eastern scriptures. In front of the gazebo, I saw my father in a sword fight with an Indian man with a beard. My father's opponent was more skillful but had no anger in his eyes; he seemed to me to just be going through the motions. My father looked desperate. I knew this man was the incarnation of Death; his sword cut down into my father's right lung and he fell. The next day I got a call from my mother, telling me that my father had just been diagnosed with cancer in his right lung.

A year later, I began having lucid dreams and what seemed like lessons. while having Out of Body Experiences (OBEs). One night I saw myself in a fight with people but in the end, there was left only the same man who represented Death in the dream of my father and me; Death and I were the last ones standing.

Soon thereafter, I noticed I could feel, from a few feet away, sore spots in people, even over the phone. If I touched those spots on their body, there was pain. If they touched them, there was not. Thoughts of chi and acupressure came to mind. When I engaged in this practice, my eyes would sometimes hurt. One time, my wife looked at me and remarked how my eyes looked like hematite, a stone with a mirror finish. I looked myself and sure enough, they did.

Of the OBEs, these were not my first. An earlier series seemed tuned into the past and future. The first saw me in Japan in the late 1500s, as a Samurai. In this time of my young life here, I was devoted to practicing the martial arts and liked Kendo, the art of the Japanese sword. Other than tennis and bicycle racing, martial arts seemed the only other thing I was naturally good at; perhaps this was why. In my vision, I was resting on top of some shelves when a bunch of other Samurai ran in and I rolled off the top and into the middle of them.

Swinging my sword, cutting back and forth, I was smiling, even knowing I was about to die. I believe I was helping people revolt against the Shogunate. Years later, I made my own suit of Samurai armor, and a friend who was working at the Metropolitan Museum of Art as an armorer gave me a book a visiting Japanese armorer gave him, on the making of arms and armor in 16th century Japan. Right there was a complicated chainmail and plate pattern I'd made for both arms, from memory, I suppose.

I had another memory of being a woman on Mars; she/I am part of a scientific settlement. I was in the medical profession and I remember seeing gurneys hovering over the floor. I remember being very purposeful and focused on my work. A strong young man who I felt was a friend and I went upstairs to my room (I think, somewhere private anyway) and my memory is I was raped by him or will be. As I have no memory beyond that, I am not sure if I died as well.

Fast forward twenty years and I found myself a Lecturer at Yale University School of Medicine, experimenting with medical devices you could wear or even swallow, destined for the International Space Station. *USA Today* said I was one of the main troopers in the emerging discipline of telemedicine. Is it possible that this experience provides the background and inclination necessary for my future female self to choose a career in, along with my across-lifetimes interest in space and planetary exploration?

Not long after I moved into my first apartment, I had a vision of having died and seeing my girlfriend at the time, now older and with a daughter, visiting a mausoleum where I was interred. I remember there was a small ledge inside with my name on a small brass plate. It had fallen over, face forward, and she propped it back up so that my name was visible. I tried telling her I was alive and well, as she was sad. But without a physical mouth, my words went unheard.

In the Fall of 1989, I had an OBE of getting onto a military helicopter in the middle of the night in the Middle East. As we took off, I stood by the big open door and saw a man in a turban spring up from behind some crates and aim a shoulder mounted missile launcher at us. He and I locked eyes. There was a brilliant white flash and after that, I glided down slowly into a neighborhood. It was dusk; there were no colors per se. I saw there was a small sign hanging around my neck, as if my life story was there for anyone who needed to know.

I walked around what was supposed to be familiar environs and looked into some of the windows. I didn't feel too attached and just accepted I was dead. I do remember going somewhere where a there was a large gathering of people I knew and trying again as I had twenty years prior, to comfort them, but to no avail. In the end, I realized the dead move on because our grief tortures them. I know this because I have seen it from the other side; visiting my own tomb to comfort a loved one who visited it or visiting my neighborhood to tell my neighbors I'm "still alive", yet without a physical body to do so, the task is impossible. You can watch your loved ones lament for only so long before you just give up and for your own sanity, move on. And back on this side, when you see the living suffer over the pain of losing someone, you have compassion for them; the living should know how hard it is for those they love who have passed on, and even then may be standing there, right next to them, torn up by the sorrow of those left behind.

One of the last OBEs I had was of being in the Middle East and blown out of the sky when taking off in a helicopter. It was realized in full when I went to Iraq in 2003. I saw my name move across a board with different military units; Army, Marines, Air Force. It settled on Marines, and stopped at Ground or Air, then moved on to Air. Then it paused at Fixed Wing or Rotary Wing and moved to Rotary Wing. Oh hell, there it was, I was going to be embedded with a Marines helicopter squadron!

I realized my vision from 13 years prior was coming to frui-tion. At that time I couldn't see how I'd ever come to the Middle East and get on a military helicopter and now here I was about to invade Baghdad and get shot down doing it. Every night when I got on the hundreds of helicopter flights over the next several months, I thought, "tonight is when I die." I am not sure what that does to a person after a while, but I just accepted it. I got on the satellite phone and made my peace with everyone. On the night of the invasion, the helicopter next to mine went down and killed everyone onboard. We pressed through and returned safely to our base just inside Kuwait. In the end, I didn't die, and I believe it was because of certain choices I made between having the vision and arriving in the Middle East. Those choices were related to marrying a widow and her three fatherless babies. I chose to be part of something greater than myself. People in church would say to Dana how lucky she was, and I'd wince, thinking how lucky *I* was- to have a family.

The other surprising experience was after the war was over. The Marines I was embedded with handed off to the Army and we went south to Al Hillah (Babylon). One day my team and I came across some mass graves. The locals were out there in force digging them up, looking for family members they hadn't seen in over 10 years. All forensic integrity was gone as they piled bones and clothes into piles and put skulls on top. Most piles were probably comprised of the skeletal remains from several people.

While I was there, I felt this sudden and strong instinct to return at night and sleep there, right among the thousands of bodies. I said as much to my Marines. They calmly asked if I was sure I wasn't a Marine, as they also think strange things like this sometimes. I knew I would not be able to do this though, as the town would be out there all night long until they felt everybody had been dug up. My trying to sleep there would, at the least, have been seen as disrespectful. I have no idea why I wanted to do this, but it felt like I wanted out of my body during sleep to comfort any of the dead who might still be hanging around.

What drove me towards those dead was compassion. OBEs were not the only experiences. Along more Shamanic lines, I was with Bill Garrett, a former editor of National Geographic magazine, in Guatemala. We were on Lake Izabal and went up a small river with really high cliffs on either side. The river was shallow but dark due to the tannin from deforestation upriver. In this middle of nowhere, I found and swam into a cave and once inside, climbed out onto a rock shelf. I stood there and listened to an underground waterfall. It was pitch black.

I suddenly felt sleepy, as I used to in university when I was studying hard, falling asleep for 20 minutes was something I did when I needed to integrate a lot of information. I felt the same need right then. I lay down and went to sleep in the cave. About 20 minutes later, I awoke and felt embraced by Mother Earth in some way; I didn't feel out of place at all in being there. I could still hear the waterfall, but now I could see small pin pricks of light in the ceiling cave. It was the forest floor outside. This was sunlight peeking through and I re-entered the water and swam out of the cave.

*Mass graves with thousands of bodies from the late 1980s/early 1990s, Hillah (Babylon), Iraq*

Chapter Five:

# Back to the Present

Coming back to the present, my effort to consider, without emotion, the experiences that brought me to this point helped view the journey as one of process - the "how" did it happen point-of-view - rather than the content or the "what" happened. This improved my insights into the In Between through the enjoyable research into what I call a consumer grade level of quantum physics.

I have always loved math and science, and one of my majors in university was physics. I woke up every morning and looked at the morning news feed of the latest science topics.

Some emerging research on time, gravity, entanglement and super-positioned probabilities caught my attention. As I followed these threads, I felt I was understanding more about my inner experience.

For instance, those gears of possible futures flowing ghostlike through each other are what quantum physics calls the super-positioning of probabilities within an emerging event. From those simultaneous waves of possibilities, eventually one will collapse to become a particle and moment in our physical reality. This is what "choice;" is; it is all about probabilities.

I mentioned some of the gears were less in focus than others. I understand now you can't fully focus on a probability because it is a representation of several possibilities. Choices offered and choices made are not in a single place but spread out unevenly over a life; the meanings of the more definite decisions are clear. Then one is chosen and supersedes the others to become the singular present. The In Between held a poetic statement; all the emerging thoughts, words and deeds, birthing from the future to the present appeared in the shape of an egg.

A key consideration of my experience was the question of time. Within my NDE, in the In Between, I was told that where I stood was inside the eternity of a single moment. It was referred to as the "Impossible Now." Impossible because the moment, the Present, is impossibly thin but expands across universes. Interestingly, it seems Lewis Carroll (Charles Lutwidge Dodgson) had an interesting insight about time too, as demonstrated in *Alice in Wonderland (1865)*:

*"How long is forever?" asks Alice.*
*"Sometimes, just one second," replies the White Rabbit.*

In quantum physics, there is a unit of time measurement called Planck Time, named after the father of quantum physics, Max Planck. It is an incredibly small length of time in which quantum events occur. Specifically, it is $10^{-43}$ seconds, or a hundred millionth of a trillionth of a trillionth of a trillionth of a second. It corresponds to the super-tiny distance in which light travels in one unit of Planck time: $1.616255 \times 10^{-35}$ meters. At these scales of time and space, classical physics falls apart.

I believe I was in the In Between this length of time while one week passed here on earth. In reconciling the two time frames, let's go back to the classical physics of Einstein. Remember $E=MC^2$? Simply put, it says that as we approach the relativistic speed of light, our mass approaches infinity, time slows down toward zero (compared to the non-relativistic place we left) and the distance between us and our target destination also approaches zero. This means that you would need all the energy in the universe to travel at light speed but if you could do that, you would instantly be everywhere there is to be in one moment, and weigh everything there is to weigh. You would have become one with the universe.

Another way of looking at this equation is that for light, there is no time. Therefore, I have wondered if in leaving our bodies, becoming more light-like and less mass-like, we perceive a change in the passage of time on higher planes. The degree to which time slows is in proportion to our light/mass ratio, an indicator of how far within and how far away from mass we have gone.

As I write this, I realize my words could be seen as self-aggrandizing; some will question my depth of travel based on how time appeared to slow. I don't want to have a pissing contest with other experiencers regarding the matter. Whether I have an ego or not, I don't have to be perfect to have a perfect, or *perfecting*, experience. Just because you are put on the path of enlightenment doesn't mean you are enlightened; you still must do the work.

The In Between shows the quantum reality of time, entanglement and how all things are interconnected. Not only across impossible distances, but across all of time. There are entangled particles that are a universe apart, but when you change the state of one, you instantly change the state of its entangled mate, no matter the distance in space or even in time. There are things that happened at the beginning of time that *are*, not will, affecting other things at the end of time. Which would mean that everything in between is already happening and all at once. Which means there is only the present, always has been and always will be.

Time is an artificial construct by which the story plays out with a beginning, middle and end. Humans crave that order.

Does this imply everything we experience is scripted? If it is, what we have to get used to is that each possible choice probability actually does spawn its own moment in time, with its own future, allowing every possibility to play out. It's our limited ability to focus on only one reality at a time that keeps us from seeing all the possibilities that come into expression simultaneously, and then see their timelines extending into the future.

Quantum physics says the observer affects the outcome of any event through the simple act of observation. Yet when every outcome is occurring, the question is not how our watching events unfold affects them, but why are any of our unique frames of references excluded from seeing any other outcomes? I guess because we are following the script of a particular timeline.

The best answers I can give as to why one timeline triumphs over another and defines our observable lives as destiny, is either free will or karma. Yes, there are both. Karma is what happens to you when you didn't plan and free will is how you choose to react to it. A deeper and personal consideration is around our alternate selves in the Multiple Universe Theory where an infinite number of ourselves spawn off every single moment to live out all the choices we didn't make. As intriguing as this possibility appears, there is no way to wrap our heads around the idea we are simultaneously incarnated yet oblivious to all our other lives. Truly, we live now and always have in the infinite worlds of maybe. Is individuality, like time, an illusion and we are as infinitely probable as everything else?

Chapter Six:

# Many Worlds Interpretation

Back in the late 1950s, **Hugh Everett III put forth the Many Worlds Interpretation.**

> *According to the many worlds view, there is no difference between a particle or system before and after it has been observed, and no separate way of evolving. In fact, the observer himself is a quantum system, which interacts with other quantum systems, with different possible versions seeing the particle or object in different positions, for example. These different versions exist concurrently in different alternative or* **parallel universes**. *Thus, each time quantum systems interact with each other, the wave function does not collapse but actually splits into alternative versions of reality, all of which are equally real.*
>
> *This view has the advantage of conserving all the information from wave functions so that each individual universe is completely deterministic, and the wave function can be evolved forwards and backwards.*
>
> http://www.exactlywhatistime.com/physics-of-time/quantum-time/ (Copyright © 2020 )

If we are indeed children of God, then there is no *re*incarnation, just one incarnation, and we're living them all out. All that we ever were or will ever be, we live at the same "time" in that present, squeezed between the ultimate beginning and ultimate end of the universes all of our selves live in. It shows how powerful our souls really are and how impossibly unknowable all this truly is, if seen only from a limited frame of reference. From within any of the universes, we can only know that individual universe. We have to rise above them all to see the pattern of how they co-exist.

A Sikh guru, Sant Sawan Singh, offered clarity in one of my favorite books, *Spiritual Gems*, first published in 1958.

*There are two ways of looking at this creation :*

1. *From the top, looking down—the Creator's point of view or*
2. *From the bottom, looking up—man's point of view.*

From the top it looks as though the Creator is all in all. He is the only Doer, and the individual seems like a puppet tossed right and left by the wire puller.

There seems to be no free will in the individual, and therefore no responsibility on his shoulder. It is His play. There is no why or wherefore. All the Saints, when They look from the top, describe the creation as His manifestation. They see Him working everywhere.

Looking from below, or the individual viewpoint, we come across Variety as opposed to Oneness. Everybody appears to be working with a *will and is influenced by and is influencing others with whom he comes in contact. The individual thinks he is the doer and thereby becomes responsible for his actions and their consequences. All the actions are recorded in his mind and memory, and cause likes and dislikes which keep him pinned down to the material, astral or mental spheres, according to his actions in an earlier life in the cycle of transmigration. The individual in these regions cannot help doing actions and, having done them, cannot escape their influences. The individual acts as the doer and therefore bears the con- sequences of his actions.*

As stated above, the observations differ on account of the difference in the angle of vision. Both are right.

The question regarding the existence of a multiverse of parallel worlds and lives keeps popping up over and over again. This image articulates the question of "what if?"

*Arjuna bows before Vishwarupa ,the Cosmic form of Krishna; sometimes also depicted with four faces: male (front, east), lion/Narasimha (south), boar/Varaha (north) and woman (back/west), Singapore.*

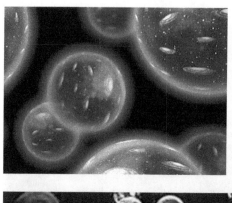
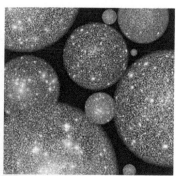

If the above describes the usual but impossible ways everything plays out moment by moment, then how do I explain what's going on in the In Between? If all realities are happening, what is there for me to change? Where were the other Jims while I was here doing this? Is there a place where we're all going to meet, in one place and in one time, in one…singularity?

I realized I was given a chance to remove choices across universes, not just my original one. I was consolidating realities to an increasingly single set of circumstances and thereby aligning the Jim path across all possible timelines, toward Home.

As I pulled out choices that felt wrong to keep, I pondered the machine's whirring around to reset the gears to futures that won't exist.

The number of realities popping out of the present is based on our own individual desires, which are many. Think of all the "what ifs"? as we decide whether to turn left or right, choose wrong or right, whether to step into the dark or the light, and every shade between. Perhaps as our desires fade, so do the number of ways we ponder them. The man with few desires is a man with few paths to walk. The man with no desire has no path to walk. In one sense, he is free and not bound by time or space; he can be everywhere there is to be, and at the same time. He can understand all the choices before us, and the fruits of each. Understanding causality from this perspective, he is also free from having to walk any more paths. He is done. *It* is done.

In seeing the resetting of the machine's gears to those cancelled futures, the lesser man would try and remember every scene of major events as they whipped by; when to buy into the stock market, or make a major real estate purchase, and when to sell, right in the nick of time to get rich. Who they would marry and when, who close to them would die and why, and on and on. These facts are answers to the big questions in life. What do I do for a living? Who will I marry? How will I die? The greater man doesn't worry about the answers because they are a one-shot deal to each parallel reality anyway. It's the *understanding*, not the answers, that threads the multiverse together. By limiting the numbers of paths the present can take, your limited understanding, by definition, is increased to include them all. It may sound like a trick, but it's how God bends the rules without breaking them.

Here is a personal example from earlier this year. One night I woke up and saw the shadows of leafless branches in sharp detail, cast upon a black wardrobe in my bedroom. It was February and the wind was blowing, causing the limbs to move violently back and forth across the furniture.

As I watched the movement, my focus changed and I saw a story playing out; the motion of the limbs was being translated into a movie or cartoon- just like we use computers to convert what appears to be a random bunch of 1s and 0s into a story with a beginning, middle and end, that's computing coding. The dancing branches appearance was like an old style black and white movie. I lay there trying to understand the story.

However, I could not. The challenge I had was to be Present. In those moments watching the tree shadows, trying to interpret any information in a linear fashion would be futile. The best analogy I can give is this: movies play at a rate of 24 or 25 frames per second; each frame a single photograph. When your present contracts to near zero time, past and future cease to have meaning, and so does the last frame you just saw because you forgot it and the next frame you can't anticipate. You simply see, not watch, the movie one frame at a time. It's impossible to derive meaning this way; we must take in information in a different way.

Others report similar experiences in the In Between; receiving information as a download instead of receiving it linearly. Again, it's like downloading a movie online that is nothing but a bunch of random appearing 1s and 0s in 3 minutes but then playing it through a media player for the next two hours in order to translate it into something intelligible.

This helped me understand why I couldn't see the individual choices I removed from the egg of my destiny, why only pain was my guide. I mentioned when I looked at the gears, I saw a video feed for each gear playing in my head of the event it represented. Honestly, they had little meaning to me because they were in my future. If I had tried to pick out which gears needed removing by using my predominant sense- sight- I would have been at a loss to do so because at that point in the experience, I couldn't have understood the beginning, the middle and the end of what the sector gears were telling me. Remember, the sector gears were important in that their design is to sweep back and forth, their motion having a beginning, middle and end like all experiences. If they were completely round, as we're used to seeing them, then where would they begin and where would they end?

But I could understand pain, whether it ran the course of the gear's arc or whether it lasted only for that Impossible Nowness of Planck Time: one hundred millionth of a trillionth of a trillionth of a trillionth of one second. While I felt humbled that pain instead of virtue was guiding my decisions in pruning my future possibilities, I see now there was little choice in terms of how I could process information within the literal time constraint of no-time.

You need time to process linear information. Without it, being in the moment, a movie or any other narrative is only a frame by frame set of pictures seen by an amnesiac. By the time they see the next frame, it's as if they have forgotten the one they are looking at now even if they could accurately describe it in full detail. This is how different I believe things are in the In Between in terms of who we really are, in terms of how we interact, perceive and process information and how challenging it must be to communicate with us during our brief visits there. Hence the download process; load us up with videos we can play back in the media players of our minds when we return home. Whether you travel over and see the In Between as I do or in another way, according to what you need and how you need it, the stories of "no time" and interconnectedness seem to support that this is how we think and perceive things (oftentimes with 360-degree vision)once we rise above the limitations of the physical body and brain.

I have experienced these differences in processing information in and out of linear time.

Somewhere in this time of quietly processing my experience and facing the challenges of integrating it into my everyday life, I began taking a drive in the mornings and evenings just to be quiet and present. I would listen to audiobooks either on quantum physics or Near-Death Experiences.

In the list I downloaded was this one title: *Near-Death Experiences, The Rest of the Story: What They Teach Us About Living and Dying and Our True Purpose*, by P.M.H. Atwater, 2011. As I drove and listened, I was immediately impressed by P.M.H.'s expertise. Was she a doctor of letters, conducting research? Or a scientist? Neither, she was the daughter of a policeman. Having grown up in a police station, she paid attention to how to interview people, watching their body language, listening to nuance, emphasis and inflection as much as to the actual words. Then she knew where to dig in and dig deep.

At one point, she spoke of something called a colloidal condition: an instance that occurs when something is momentarily suspended between imploding and exploding. She said this condition occurs when people are in car crashes or suffer from falls. My ears perked up. I replayed that portion of the audio and paid closer attention. As P.M.H. further explained, the details of a colloidal condition and the particles making them are called colloids, the notion that once our bodies, minds and spirits, once having been in that condition will forever carry that imprint almost made me stop the car. When I heard these words in her audiobook, it was like catching a life preserver as I was drowning. I pulled over to the side of the road and played it again.

She continued:

*A colloidal condition is a peculiar in-between state that occurs when forces suddenly collapse and then converge. This in-between state creates anti-force, which is antigravity. Particles caught in this unique state between implosion and explosion transmute and remain forever changed by that transmutation. On a molecular level, these particles show evidence of enlargement and of having taken on different and enhanced characteristics.*

And bringing in my experience's attributes is the suspended time and depersonalization aspects:

*The same thing can happen to the human brain if suddenly hit, jarred, or severely jiggled, especially during an automobile accident or as a result of a fall. Typically a colloid-like suspension of consciousness will follow such trauma, whereby the environment appears to expand out as time slows to a standstill. The individual feels somehow caught in between realities when this occurs, as if he or she has slipped through a crack in time and space and suddenly become resident of a world neither here nor there. This peculiar feeling of being suspended in between realities affects a person so deeply that it can permanently alter the way the individual regards the world at large and his or her place in it. Of interest is that consciousness, even if simply released from the bias of thought as in a flow state or during meditation, will behave somewhat the same way. Also of interest is another state, termed the "acute dying experience," that produces "peritraumatic dissociation."*

*Described medically as depersonalization in the face of life-threatening danger, the acute dying experience occurs when one's sense of time ceases at the same time that profound feelings of unreality and hyperarousal occur—as well as out-of-body experiences, decreased pain perception, disconnection from body, disorientation, tunnel vision, dissociation, numbness, and dreamlike states. This state, although tossed around in near-death circles as a possible corollary, doesn't fit research, mine or anyone else's.*

That line isn't meant to be dismissive of the "possible corollary."
P.M.H. is simply saying it is so unique and unusual that they
haven't yet found a place to put it. But in describing it at all, she
describes my own NDE in one sentence; she's as right and true
as anyone anywhere else unpacking the experience. Then P.M.H.
referred to the Void, and my experience falls exactly In Between
both of these aspects:

> *The Void appears in both uplifting and distressing near-death experi-
> ence,. not often, but sometimes. But it is always described with a type
> of emotion that is distinct. If connected with a hellish or frightening
> near-death state, the fear that is experienced can border on or become
> utmost terror; all-consuming, almost irrational. Being in a void is
> like being in a nothing state, either dark or colorless, where you are
> alone—no sounds, no movement, no objects, no being-ness, no top or
> bottom, no sides—and left with a sense of abandonment. This can
> be experienced as the ultimate condemnation. There are no demons
> and dungeons, no punishment that can compare to this feeling.*
>
> *Individuals who experience this type of frightening void find
> it difficult to describe, as if it were something they want to forget.
> Conversely, voids that appear as components of pleasant and transcen-
> dent episodes inspire a certain awe that such a place even exists. This
> pleasant void is most often described as being the central source/place
> of everything—yet devoid of all, save a sense of thrill or shimmer
> as if the void were Creation's Womb, pregnant this "invitation to
> produce" as somehow connected to our thoughts and attitudes, as if
> our state of consciousness is important to what issues forth. This type
> of void is described as a dark space that isn't dark, an emptiness that
> really isn't empty. Mystics, monks, and spiritual folk speak of the
> void in this manner, as if it were a special place they feel privileged
> to visit in deep prayer or meditation.*

At this point, P.M.H. referenced the "In Between" and afterwards, many times in the remainder of her book. Whereas I had referenced the Impossible Now, she referred to the Eternal Now.

*Let's look at this issue yet another way: Distressing experiences —encountering one's shadow and whatever aspect of self has been repressed or denied. Radiant experiences —a reunion with one's authenticity and worthiness, equally repressed and or denied. The world around us exists as perceived because of how perceived. We are real. Our world is real. What happens to us is real. Slip in between the varied aspects of this realness . . . and everything changes.*

***In Between/Suspension****: Traditionally referred to as "unifying with total Oneness." Sanctity of all sanctity is said to be encountered here—a luminous experience of all knowing, all love, all joy, all peace—with the Source of All Being.*

*Typical Experience: Any imagery or abstracts are temporary and quickly dissolve once the experiencer is at ease—instant illumination, enlightenment, music sweeps, brilliance, God/Allah/Deity.*

*The In Between is considered that which contains and embraces and unifies all—the realm of the super-conscious mind—where everything becomes more of itself as it converges back into the collective whole. Actually devoid of color, the In Between is said to be a network of luminous shimmer.*

Finally, I found someone who was from the same planet! We spoke in the same terms learned within to describe the same experience and place. I'd come to feel that in a one in a million population, I was a smaller percentage of even that. With this, I knew P.M.H. and I were connected and friends already. I sent her an email and we setup a time to call.

Because this was in February and I knew I would need a meditative drive after, I started my car to warm it up before calling her. Our conversation was easy and comfortable. At 4:40 pm, I felt my state of energy change. It came without warning or prompting- it just happened. It was an upward nudge of being more alert and present, not like a Kundalini awakening or anything dramatic as that. I didn't say anything because it was that gentle but right then, P.M.H. said, "Our energies are melding." I told her I could feel it.

We talked more about being Present and the Impossible/ Eternal Now in which time stops. We wrapped up our call at 5:00 PM and I walked out to my warmed-up car for my drive. As I looked at the porch light, it blew out. I quietly laughed to myself and got into the car. The clock in the radio was showing the normal time as I expected. The other clock, in my console, was frozen on 4:40 PM, and it stayed that way my entire drive. I thought it funny I had two time zones represented in my car, normal and In Between time. When I returned home an hour later, I restarted the car and both clocks were synched and reporting the "correct" time.

And after all this, people still ask me, "how do you know it wasn't a hallucination?

Chapter Seven:

# We're not in Kansas Anymore: After Effects

When you share your NDE with some people, they will ask how you know it was real and not a hallucination. With enough time and beating down by a disbelieving social circle, there may come a time when you ask yourself the same question.

One of the best responses I've heard is there is a randomness to hallucinations. There are no two hallucinations that present the same attributes as so many NDEs do. Hallucinations are more random and no one has reported an NDE where God told them to be a serial killer.

Coming back isn't easy, even on a good day. You have the psychological after-effects of an NDE; 65-78% of experiencers divorce. Their openness and increased empathy post-NDE bring accusations of flirtations and emotional adultery. Their sense of time and attachment to money and power disappear, as well as other indicators that their values have changed at the core. People attempt to explain it away by saying "people get divorced every day, or are tossing in the professional towel, or going through mid-life crises or other changes." Sadly, the world at large has weak explanations in the dramatic changes in the NDEer.

There are other after-effects that can be less ignored, undeniable phenomena such as electrical and electronic interference, light bulbs blowing out, computers going haywire and digital watches failing to keep time.

From the IANDS webpage, there is a lot of helpful information to understand the NDE as an experiencer, a caregiver or partner or a researcher.

IANDS.ORG/NDES/COMMON AFTEREFFECTS:

---

### *Electrical Phenomena:*

*Electrical sensitivity refers to a condition whereby the force field or energy around an individual affects nearby electrical equipment and technological devices. Usually sporadic in effect and impact, some experiencers have noticed: watches can stop, microphones "squeal," tape recorders quit, television channels change with no one at controls, light bulbs pop, telephone "drops off," computers suddenly lose memory, and so forth.*

In a period of six months, along with a constant changing of blown light bulbs, I had to replace my central air system and four of five damper motors in the ductwork that direct airflow. Installers reviewed the situation for a day and all they could come up with was a "power surge".

One day my stepson Brian and I went for a drive. When we returned home, I got out of the car first and put my aluminum travel mug on the top of his car as I waited for him to collect his things.

As soon as I put the cup on the roof, it began to shake as if it were in an earthquake. I knew this was weird and listened for an engine fan which is in some cars and runs for a few minutes after the engine is turned off. There was none. The cup was rattling around all on its own. I knew if I told Brian to stand up and see it, it would break the spell and stop. I stood there for one or two minutes, wishing he'd hurry up and worried I'd be the only one to see it. Finally, he stood up and looked at the jiggling cup, then at me and back at the cup again. It showed no signs of slowing down or stopping. I again asked him if he was sure his engine didn't have some type of cooling fan, anything to explain the vibration of the cup. He assured me there was nothing in his car making this happen. I picked the cup up and sat it back down. Nothing. We had just been talking about NDEs and the In Between during our drive, so I chalked it up to that. We went inside and I poured my remaining coffee, now cooled down, into a ceramic cup and put it in the microwave for the usual thirty seconds. During this time, Brian and I talked about the weirdness of the dancing cup. When the microwave oven beeped the coffee's readiness 30 seconds later, I reached inside. As soon as I touched the mug, the coffee exploded in all directions. It wasn't hotter than you'd expect after 30 seconds so I knew I didn't absentmindedly put it in for four or five minutes (to reach an explosive temperature). The microwave was completely fried and I had to replace it.

A few weeks later, I walked into five different stores on five consecutive days and their cash registers shut down every time. The next week, I was visiting my mother in North Carolina and the same thing happened with the cash register in a hardware store. I asked when it had stopped working and it was right when I walked in. When I returned to my mother's home, I told her about all of these after-effects and about the In Between in general. As I spoke, suddenly a large transformer outside her condo blew; it was a loud "boom". I asked her how often this happened and she said, "never". She called a friend to talk about it, using her POTS ("Plain Old Telephone Service - copper wire") phone, the kind that *always* works, and it failed after a minute or so and so did her friend's. Their phones didn't work for the next hour. A POTS phone with its older copper wire technology almost never goes down but these did, on a nice, sunny day.

Computers behaved in particularly strange ways after my time in the In Between. I experienced everything from computers running slow to software spontaneously opening and closing. Documents would simply disappear from the screen. I recently started working onsite with a customer of mine and one morning

I was working on both their computer and my computer, using my iPhone as a hot spot; I was therefore on a totally different network. A new friend I'd made walked up to say hello and all of a sudden both computers started going crazy and so did my phone. As I was trying to prepare for an important conference call, with some frustration I simply said, "this is due to my NDE!" and he said, "I know." I asked him how he knew and he said, "I died as a baby". This points to an amplification of effects when two or more experiencers are together.

An NDE friend of mine was driving to her boyfriend's one evening and began texting me from her phone also while listening to music on it. As I texted back, she responded her audio suddenly went haywire. We kept texting and as she walked into her boyfriend's home, *his* audio system suddenly went wonky. He yelled out with a laugh, "tell Jim to stop it!," as he knew well how when I visited the lights flickered constantly. Her son called her, as he was on break from university, and visiting her apartment. He reported the audio system in her apartment was going crazy, even in the headphones. As I shared this with my wife in real time, she became very quiet. Then I was reminded that on the moment her husband died in a highway accident a year before we met, the stereo system at their home suddenly turned on, volume full up, as if between radio stations, blaring white noise. It was just after midnight and she jumped out of bed, ran downstairs to turn it off, then unable to determine why it happened, returned to bed. The police knocked on her door about half an hour later, delivering the news that changed her and the children's lives. She remembered and now made the connection between the time of her husband's death and the radio suddenly turning on.

I referenced the amplification of some effects when two or more NDE'ers are together. Phenomena especially occurs when they are focused on their inner experience. I cited two small examples but, when the Crowne Plaza Convention Center in King of Prussia, Pennsylvania, hosted the 2019 IANDS national conference, I noticed there was a hold up in the line at Registration. When I got to the desk, I asked what was up. The woman checking people in said that the hotel's credit card readers had all gone down. I asked when and she said that it first occurred in the morning and she had no idea what caused it or when it would come back. I jokingly remarked that it was "us"- the NDE'ers checking in and that this sort of thing happens a lot. She looked at me with a confused concerned look. I assured her I was serious.

She became so intrigued that she actually came out from behind the desk and we stood to the side because she wanted to know more. As I explained additional and similar after-effects and some of my experiences, she put her hand on my arm and said, "I have the chills". I said, "yeah, that happens too". I went to the conference's check in table and told them what happened. Susan Amsden the IANDS Business Manager, was working at the table said that she was the first to check in that day, around 7:30 AM and that was when the system went down. We laughed and I made a joke it was like a hackers' convention; everything starts acting strange; elevators, lighting, audio systems, anything electrical Over the few days of the conference, attendees noticed the key card system acted up continuously; one time I had to swipe my card 10 times before it would open my door, and this was a nice hotel and conference center.

I believe the power of one's NDE, when shared with a group of experiencers who are supportive and eager, can have an amplified effect. What you experienced over on the other side comes through. People feel your peace, your sense of connectivity, your joy, whatever you've brought back. It's like bringing a bucket of "it" from the Beyond and doling it out in cups for everyone to drink. I believe now this also happened when the In Between settled into me during my hospital stay and why people were so unbelievably kind during my convalescence there.

It is easy to wonder if there is an emotional state that corresponds to all of this. When these types of anomalies occur with NDE'ers, were they experiencing any heightened emotions? This is a natural question because that's how Hollywood would portray it; you get angry and lights pop, cars are tossed around and the bad guys die. I have found no corresponding emotion to associate with these phenomena. The only possible pattern I believe I have seen, and it warrants further investigation, is these things happen when I talk about the In Between, or even recount my experience there. Times like these are when I *feel* it in the room, other people do as well (as I might not say anything but right when I get a wave of it through me, they remark on their own that they feel it). By a combination of focusing on the experience of being There and taking "me" out of the equation as much as I can – remember, I was depersonalized in the In Between -- I become a conduit for the In Between- and that's when the electrical craziness happens. Part of "what now?" in my post NDE world is to see if this is true for other experiencers, if it represents a discernable pattern and what the pattern tells us and if it has any predictive value when the attributes are re-created. If we can show *that*, then I think we will have risen our understanding considerably. I would suppose one would set up conditions to reveal changes in the environment when people share their NDE experience, especially connecting to it with their emotions and "seeing" it all over again.

Having said all this, the only emotion I can remember having when electrical anomalies occur is *annoyance*- with a person or situation. When a credit card machine at a hotel after a 7-hour drive is down, I get annoyed.

And here's a weird one- electronic messaging.

*A Facebook message that typed itself*

*2 merged emails 11 years apart, though about spiritual topics.*

The text message on the left was from an NDE friend who suddenly thought to text me when I was 20 minutes away from P.M.H. Atwater's home. I was driving and the messaging app suddenly popped up. As my friend typed, all of a sudden my own blank text field began to fill in with letters. To be one hundred percent honest, I was so startled I almost went off the road, grabbing my phone to delete the message because I had no idea what was going on, what it was about to say next, and if it would send my friend something terribly wrong for which there was no defense. I took a screen grab before deleting and still have no idea who typed it, or whether it was intended for my friend or me. I told P.M.H. (and my friend, later) about it and she laughed, saying, "this is just the beginning".

The email on the right came shortly after, from Viktoria, a European researcher. This was her second email to me. Or was it? Note the date of 3/10/19. The email begins with "Happy 2008!" and was sent by my first wife 11 years prior, in response to my asking where I might find other fellow followers of our spiritual path in the northeastern USA. I have asked a lot of really smart people in the IT world, those with the highest Cisco certifications in Unified Communications, and they have no answer as to how these two emails could have come together and merged. It's interesting both are spiritually related. What was this all about?

The psychic stuff, for want of a better description, came with greater force than ever. Remember back to my experience on the school bus, seeing the girl who went to my school appear and act differently than usual?

Dana is in the business of leasing jets to people who can afford to fly private. In December 2018, her office had a holiday party at a hip restaurant located at the airport near their offices. She invited our three children, then nineteen, twenty-one and twenty-two. As with most parents, Dana told the kids to dress up and be on their best behavior.

On the day of the party, the children drove separately, as their busy social lives meant there were other seasonal parties to attend later that evening and they would need to independently come and go. As I backed into the parking space, I noticed a young woman walking across the parking lot toward us. I remarked to Dana, "that is a very put together looking young lady". Dana thought I was making a half-hearted joke because it was Fionna, our youngest. I didn't recognize her, thinking she was someone from Dana's office walking over to say hello! It was only when we got out of the car and walked inside that her appearance "settled down" into the one I knew.

Inside, we made the rounds saying hello to everyone. Brian, our twenty-one-year-old son arrived and he and I sat downstairs near the food, chatting and people-watching. He was sitting next to me and decided to grab some food. When he returned a couple of minutes later, he sat across from me. I didn't recognize him. I remember studying his face and bone structure, thinking he was a nice-looking young man, but was somewhat affronted by this stranger's casualness with me. I was in Observer mode the entire time, with no real reaction. My feelings regarding his familiarity were a little surprising and my Observer side thought it an interesting response. Then Brian's appearance returned to the one I knew.

A few months later, in May, Dana got a lead role in a community play. She was a New York-trained actress, so this was a return to something she loved. On the night of her premiere, Fionna, Brian and I arrived early at the theater to ensure our front row seats and to meet Dana and cheer her on. As we stood outside the venue, Dana parked across the street and walked up the sidewalk toward us, carrying her clothes for the various scenes. At this time, though I intellectually knew this must be Dana, I didn't recognize her. I just observed her, and honestly, I thought "she's hot". But her appearance was shifting, at one time she looked Italian, at another, Spanish (She is a mix of Lebanese and Irish). During this time I didn't lose recognition of Brian and Fionna, so I doubt it was a stroke or a temporary case (if there is such a thing) of Prosopagnosia, or face blindness. Everyone was laughing and excited and Fionna crossed the road to help Dana with her armful of clothing. I stood neither doing nor saying anything but just smiling and wondering when she was going to settle down into the Dana I knew. Eventually, the shape shifting began to incorporate a flash or two of the woman I'd been married to for fifteen years.

Then she went inside the theater's office, speaking to the Director.

This happened a few more times, including most recently at the IANDS conference in Pennsylvania.

In every case, I felt this was due to my NDE although I haven't read about it in the experiences of others. That left me to focus deeply on each instance and look for a common pattern.

My empathy, remember, this seemed to be my superpower, was my key to understanding these three strange experiences where my daughter, my son and my wife all appeared to change appearance, then returned to normal again. Everyone else in the same environment stayed the same. The pattern consistent across all three cases consists of the following:

1.  Everyone was in a heightened energy state.
     b.  The two kids were at my wife's holiday party thrown by her office so they had to dress up and be on their best behavior, meaning they had to be "grown up." An hour before the play began, my wife walked to her first acting gig in years, excited about returning to something she truly loves.
2.  Everyone had to project someone other than who they are.
     b.  The children had to project a grown-up image to my wife's colleagues, powered by their heightened states of energy. With her heightened energy state, my wife already projected the characters she had to be in a few minutes.

This pattern, consistent across all of these instances as well as others not detailed here, tell me empathy can do more than just read a person's emotional state and inner world, it can *see* the manifestations as projections of the people who own them. It would be safe to assume the crafting of what I saw had some subjective elements to it but at the same time, have you ever tried to imagine a face you've never seen? Ideally, my mind would have been disassociated enough to not color the experience but see it as objectively as possible and without bias.

I'm curious who else this has happened to, as empathy is one of the biggies NDE'ers experience as a common psychological after-effect. If you weren't psychic before, you may well be after and if you are before the event, you are more so after. Believe me, many more questions pop up in my analysis of this experience, such as "what do the differences between the two images, the familiar and the short-term face, mean? Do the differences provide diagnostic value between the individual's inner and outer worlds?"

This constant head-scratching defines the daily work of Integration and the NDE'ers constant change. New insights and expiring attachments change the answer to my, and many NDE'ers, constant question, "who am I now and what am I becoming?"

Chapter Eight:

# Where Am I and Who Are All These People?

The after-effects of a NDE upon daily life create a ping pong effect between taking in what comes next and going back to the NDE to prospect more understanding from it. This defines the Integration or "Coping" phase.

Waking up from an NDE into a sleep-walking world creates definite challenges. Finding others like ourselves also working through this transition helps.

We feel we don't belong to our own selves because we no longer belong to that which we once thought we were: our desires and our fears.

I reflected on how interesting it was that a one week experience defined by clear memory and clear-headed, non-linear thought could be book-ended by amnesia, physical shock, daily six-hour doses of anesthesia and intense painkillers.

In other ways, my experience defied an easy explanation. I decided to see if talking to a therapist might help, if not in providing answers, at least perspective.

After a couple of tries, I realized I had no idea exactly what type of therapeutic approach was best. I tried several and found those who tried to stuff me into some box defined by their school of psychology proved fruitless. As quickly as they could, they thought they had enough data points to announce something that would indicate they were now ahead of it, only to be flat wrong. I'd explain why and they would get quiet again. It became apparent that we were simply not on the same wavelength.

I stopped going altogether, for the simple reason there was nothing wrong with me. I found myself *most* integrated when I shared my experience with others. The lesson I've learned is when I do this, I'm getting out of the way and the IB is coming through; it brings its own healing, or should I say, improved sense of adjustment. An NDE removed you from the herd so it makes sense your healing will come more from the other side than here. It is mostly a solitary path, but it doesn't have to be lonely.

Walk with people who accept that *you* believe in the experience. Walk with people who are without judgment. Let them walk alongside you, listening and offering their perspectives, sometimes as questions rather than absolutist, conversation-killing statements. A heavy-handed pronouncement like, "well in my NDE, Jesus said..." shuts down even tiptoeing into greater understanding. But framing what Jesus said into a question such as, "I wonder what God would say about that?" or "what informs your opinion or feelings on that?" allows you to, in truth, walk side by side with a companion.

Should you find kindred spirits to share your experience with, don't be surprised if you meet, hit it off, part ways for a while, and don't stay in touch. I think this is because when NDE'ers share, they are using different communication tools than non-experiencers. Yes, you walk and talk but there are also behind the scenes, downloads of information occurring with the new ability/trait of processing information outside of linear time. You still feel connected to the other person even though a long time passes because it is common for experiencers to have a different sense of time than everyone else. Once you've stepped into the Impossible Now, time is never to be the same.

Post-NDE, the first and natural place to dig is the internet. When I returned home after the hospital stay, I opened up my browser and first typed in "Purgatory" because I thought perhaps this was where I went given the gothic look of the place. When I finally realized I had indeed had a Near-Death Experience that wasn't necessarily in Purgatory but looked like it did for reasons I have explained, I downloaded audio books and books on quantum physics. I went back to more NDE's and that's where I came across P.M.H. Atwater. I readily admit after hearing many NDE experiences and reading them online, I grew weary of their similar references. I wanted more.

In part, my quest was answered as the story-telling went from the experience itself to the after-effects that followed, certainly as points of validation. But I wasn't conducting healing, talking to dead people or otherwise glowing in the dark, as I jokingly called this phase. The electrical anomalies at the time weren't apparent, and my only "proof" was the fact that I was 100% aware I was looking at this world and everyone in it more from "there" than "here".

In fact, one day my wife and I sat in the living room on our respective laptops. She researched some interior design ideas as I wrote up my experience, with its daily additional layers of depth and clarity. I didn't want to miss a detail. She saw something of interest and began talking to me, reading aloud from a webpage. I paused my work and looked up at her. She looked into my eyes and jumped with a small fright. *She saw something.* I believe she saw the In Between in my eyes. She immediately recomposed herself and denied anything happened. Right then I realized that the In Between isn't a place you go to or come from, it is simply a place you *are.*

Soon I grew weary of the "gifts" people asked about, symbolic of their spiritual transformation, especially as this aspect of the overall experience wasn't part of mine. What *was* part of my experience, the core part, were the changes in me that had to do with who I was becoming- changes in my values, my detachment from everything, and so on. I realized that in most of the media on NDEs, many were the tales of tunnels, dead loved ones, life reviews, angelic beings, and then the list of superpowers that followed one's return. Few people asked, "Tell me the wisdom you brought back". That was what I hungered for the most. What if your superpower isn't the typical psychic manifestation but a super-connection to the other side? A connection that sees everything here for what it is? Being quiet, being present, being detached...none of these are showy abilities likely to get much press. So, in a way, having not felt like I fit into society before I had an NDE, I feel even more so afterwards. I don't despair because I also feel our interconnectedness with more people now, especially among the NDE population.

This realization brought me back to my conversation with the In Between during my NDE. There are a few things I'd like to expand on or associate with some interesting quotations:

*"This is the future birthing into the now."*
*"You are in the In Between."*
*"The Impossible Now between the past and the future."*
*"It's impossible in its short duration. Yet here you are, standing inside the eternity of a single moment."*
*"Do you remember who you are in the world to which your body belongs?"*
*"Then you see the truth in how the past is dust".*

What do I make of these statements? Inside the egg were long stemmed sector gears, which pivoted from invisible anchor points in the air. Arcs of movement were expressed from those anchor points of rotation. The gears themselves varied in how in-focus they were, but their meanings were crystal clear. Sector gears are a partial arc of a gear, designed to sweep back and forth only so far. Sector gears therefore have a beginning, middle and end to their range of travel- just like the thoughts, words and actions we choose. They are found in clocks, making their appearance in a representation of my future all the more logical, ticking down one second at a time, or ready to. The gears also passed through each other, ghostlike and representing the uncertainty remaining between choosing one thing or another, how multiple choices may have common touch points, indicating how a decision made in a single moment can result in many different outcomes

I was told that this is how the present comes into being, with many possible choices presented before us, moment by moment, and it's our decision that collapses one among them into what we call "reality".

*"This is the process of Becoming."*

My fingers brush one of the more solid appearing gears. As I touch it, within my mind I see something like a video feed of future events. Then I double over in pain.

*"As far as classical Buddhism is concerned, impermanence is the number one inescapable, and essentially painful, fact of life. It is the singular existential problem that the whole edifice of Buddhist practice is meant to address."*

Norman Fischer, *Impermanence is Buddha Nature April, 2019*

*"If I'm not who I think I am, who am I? This view sees our identity as static, and hence sees us as a* **being**....

*The paradigm of simply being burdens and constrains our lives as it deprives us of a fuller and richer participation with life. It is absent the deeper meaning to be found in the evolving worldview of* **becoming.**"

Mel Schwartz, *Psychology Today, From Being to Becoming March, 2009*

*"The universe is always waiting for us to respond. It is our respon-sibility to focus on what we want in the journey of our becoming.*

*In our process of becoming we have to be aware of our choices and what energy we are putting out into the world. We live in an ongoing process of responsive conversations with the universe."*

Terrell Washington Anansi, The Good Men Project,
*Living in the Process of Becoming February 2018*

After emerging from the In Between, I see Becoming as non-per-manence. The greater our attachment to the transient, the more painful it is when that attachment is broken.

I sensed the more solid, more in-focus, gears indicate a greater certainty regarding their manifestation as choices to be made. I further sensed that in comparison to the more commonly described life review where events of the past are seen, experienced and even re-lived, this model presents future choices as an alternate to the life review.

All choices in our future were sourced in decisions we made in our past. The pain from bad choices is knowable, whether latent as it swirls around or manifest as the eventual fruit of a decision made. It's an early warning system and comes due once chosen.

Why is a life review important? If we personalize the experi-ence, we may feel guilt for all of our bad decisions or even our good fortune. If we depersonalize the experience, we have a chance to see the underlying characteristics that grant more insight into why these decisions were made in the first place; as a reaction to hurt, in hopes of a promise, in avoidance of pain, in repayment of a debt or attachment to unfinished business or desires. Ultimately, our certainty of right or wrong is always a variable because *we* get in the way.

*"I am not what happened to me. I am what I choose to become."*
Carl Jung, CW 11, Para 39 – Bollingen Series, 1970

Which model presents the most actionable intelligence? Even in the Bible, God derides the notion of atonement. You can't atone for your past, but you can make better decisions in the future. Countless sacrifices are made to apologize for evil done and yet evil remains. Shocked, people ask, "Why does God permit evil to exist?" You might as well ask, "Why doesn't God just kill off mankind?" Even today, people make false sacrifices as a promise against doing evil just before they go out and do it again. The fact you even think about it as something to avoid means that it has taken root in your mind, awaiting the right season in which to grow. Even as early as in the book of Genesis, it is written that God released the Flood in order to wipe the slate clean and start over. How long did it take man to repopulate the earth and catch up to pre-flood debauchery?

As long as there is the mind, there will be the propensity for evil. But there will also be the opportunity to become one with God. This was the choice God gave Adam and Eve. They could live in spiritual innocence, or eat of the Tree of Knowledge, take on the Mind, and now distinguish between good and evil. It's still a moment by moment decision. Having bitten the fruit, it's easier to find God than to become a Man.

*"Each gear is the probability of a thought, word or action in your future. Your destiny is resetting itself around what you have removed."*

*"Horror vacui", "Nature abhors a vacuum";*
     Aristotle, 300 BCE, Greece.

*"All choices have unintended consequences, some unfortunate and some not. The pain each brings is your guide."*

*"What Einstein called "spooky" action at a distance could theoretically be evidence of retrocausality, which is the particle equivalent of you getting a stomach ache today thanks to tomorrow's bad lunch."*

Mike McRae, ScienceAlert.Com, June 2018

*"There are downsides to everything; there are unintended consequences to everything."*

Steve Jobs, Rolling Stone, December 2003

*"It is…highly probable that from the very beginning, apart from death, the only ironclad rule of human experience has been the Law of Unintended Consequences."*

Ian Tattersall, Masters of the Planet: The Search for Our Human Origins, March 2012

*"You're not here to feel good."*

*"The sage is ready to use all situations and doesn't waste anything. This is called embodying the light."*

Lao Tzu, 600 BCE, China.

*"To rank the effort above the prize may be called love."*

Confucius, 500 BCE, China.

*"Eliminating bad choices doesn't mean you won't make wrong ones. You won't know they are wrong until after they pass. Since right and wrong are variables over which you have no control, the answers to what comes tomorrow are a waste. Better is understanding the beauty of how everything fits and re-fits together."*

*"There is a Taoist story of an old farmer who had worked his crops for many years. One day his horse ran away. Upon hearing the news, his neighbors came to visit. "Such bad luck," they said sympathetically.*

*"Maybe," the farmer replied.*

*The next morning the horse returned, bringing with it three other wild horses. "How wonderful," the neighbors exclaimed.*

*"Maybe," replied the old man.*

*The following day, his son tried to ride one of the untamed horses, was thrown, and broke his leg. The neighbors again came to offer their sympathy for what they called his "misfortune."*

*"Maybe," answered the farmer.*

*The day after, military officials came to the village to draft young men into the army. Seeing that the son's leg was broken, they passed him by. The neighbors congratulated the farmer on how well things had turned out.*

*"Maybe," said the farmer.*

*The Taoist Farmer literally does not care what happens. He doesn't divide Life into good events and bad events, like piles of laundry. He experiences Life as one thing: undifferentiated energy/consciousness."*

Requoted by: Tao: *The Watercourse Way*,

by Alan Watts January 1977

*"So what am I missing here, in my lack of understanding?"*

*"What is clearly before you. Grace. No one deserves salvation- it can only be given by Grace.*

*It is your birthright, but it must be chosen, at the expense of the world that separates us."*

*"The life of money-making is one undertaken under compulsion, and wealth is evidently not the good we are seeking; for it is merely useful and for the sake of something else."*

Aristotle, 300 BCE, Greece.

*"When you are inspired by some great purpose, some extraordinary project, all your thoughts break their bonds."*

Patanjali, 100 BCE, India.

*"One time a man looking for a guru, met one and asked if it was true that our destiny is written upon our foreheads. The guru surprisingly answered yes, this was true. The would-be disciple then asked, "So why then do we need you?" The guru instructed him that while each man's destiny is written upon his head and in his palm, God's Grace is written upon no one, it is for the Lord to give."*

Sar Bachan, Swami Ji Maharaj, 1818-1878

*"This fixing my future is painful. I feel ashamed that I'm not doing it with some moral compass. I'm only guided by pain. I don't even know where or when these futures happen."*

*"Where is no more important than what or when. Removing your enthusiasm to further chain yourself to the world isn't as painful as carrying the crushing weight of those chains, once forged around you."*

*"Most powerful is he who has himself in his own power."*

Seneca, 4BCE – AD65, Rome.

*"If those with choices make poor use of them, then offering fewer possibilities could be called mercy. "*

*"Although you may spend your life killing, you will not exhaust all your foes. But if you quell your own anger, your real enemy will be slain."*
Nagarjuna, 200 CE, India.

*"The wealth required by nature is limited and is easy to procure; but the wealth required by vain ideals extends to infinity."*
Epicurus, 300 BCE, Greece.

*"You can't change the past. But you can make better choices in the future. Everything is interconnected. And pay more attention to your relationships. Be gentle with everyone, as I am gentle with you."*

*"The people who are crazy enough to think they can change the world are the ones who do."*
Rob Siltanen, Siltanen & Partners, for the
Apple "Think Different" campaign, 1997

*"Gentle? What's gentle about all this?"*

*"You prayed for something for which being here is the answer. And now the man who fell from the sky is not the same who flew into it."*

*"No man ever steps in the same river twice, for it's not the same river and he's not the same man."*
Heraclitus, 500 BCE, Ephesus, (Turkey)

It's like looking in a mirror of Truth with no filters of ego to soften the reflection of ourselves to ourselves. There is a humbling intimacy to the experience which continues to unfold as part of the integration phase for years after. Imagine being stripped naked in some world's Times Square for all to see; they could see your every weakness and only then were you given your superpower.

You would walk differently than others every day after yet not for the reasons most think.

Part of the integration process is to understand whether the NDE was in fact a quantum leap from the way you lived your life before, or if seen from a different perspective, was it the most natural next step in your evolution?

At this point, my outer world is one of continual adjustment congruent with my seeing how differently things appear and my deep change of values. I understand now that much of my spiritual understanding pre-NDE was intellectual whereas now it is woven into the fabric of my being. Before, my response in some related discussion came from quoting others. Now they come from, or through, me.

Chapter Nine:

# Thoughts and Reflections

Upon return from your NDE and integrating it into your life on earth, you begin coping. You notice your attachments have less glue and now you struggle with detachment; your relationships struggle with it too. With your attachments cut at their roots, you can accelerate their expiration through greater activity with them, or you can slow down their demise by delaying your interaction with them. But the total duration of time (amount of karma, perhaps?) you will spend with them probably remains about the same.

As they fall away, you ask yourself, "what do I do now?" You ask yourself because you once identified with those disappearing things. If any new attachments/habits replace them, they don't seem to have the staying power as they had before- so they run out of gas quickly and you move on. It makes sense, doesn't it?

Intensity binds us to a sense of self. That's why war veterans (beyond the explanation of PTSD) jump into bushes if a car backfires, why people return to terrible relationships and the like Likewise, the Intensity and the Timelessness of an NDE re-roots us from Here to There. In short, as your attachment to things here draws to a close and therefore gives life a different meaning, the emptiness left by those dying attachments leaves you no choice but to form a new attachment to the sublime. For me, I have no interest in old hobbies and very little interest in establishing new ones. I'm an introvert and now I feel more self-contained, so I don't get lonely. I work and find myself spending less time with other family members who are engaged in their own busy days and nights. I am not complaining, and I don't mean to sound depressed. I'm simply wrapping things up in this life in preparation for the next. If you have experienced an NDE, you'll understand my meaning. If you haven't, I doubt there are words to explain.

Melting attachments was part of realizing how I had been removed from the herd and redefined by a powerfully intense but de-personalizing experience. I can still engage with people, and they find me likable, but there is no "glue" now. Even if someone pisses me off, I forget it quickly. I feel like I'm skating along, waiting to see what materializes. I'm sure the world would have a hundred ways to describe this as a pathology, but mystical writings say this is right. An old Bushman in Namibia once told me, "sometimes the best way to hunt is to sit and wait." Decoupling from the world can be summed up like this: If your heart is full of the world, where is there room for God?

I don't miss "the old Jim" though maybe some do. One of the symptoms that proved this is when NDEers tell their stories. They almost forget to share the usually awful circumstances that created the opportunity for their NDE to occur. The life-threatening accident or terminal illness became a footnote in the story; whereas without the NDE, they themselves would *be* the story. The result is the difference between wanting to never be sick again versus becoming unafraid of death.

I feel like I am slowly becoming more of the person who was on the Other Side- not defined as much by personality or attachments, clinging less to memories of my past or anticipation of things to come. I am just present, within the Impossible Now. At least I have some of the weird after-effects with electronics to remind me that I'm not nuts.

You can see the challenge in talking to a counselor about this, because if they haven't had an NDE or are NDE-friendly, you quickly realize you're wasting your breath after about two minutes. Their art is to look and listen through the lens of the training of

their school of therapy; you know, the "to a man with a hammer…"
saying. But your experience doesn't fit tidily into the compartment
their school needs to understand it. The NDE doesn't even fit into
the scientific method, because it's not a phenomenon that can be
measured in and of itself, only its effects. Nor is it reproducible or
predictive. The checklist of after effects and a community in which
to share our integration challenges are the closest things we have
for guidance as to what's happening now and what comes next.

On that note, making friends with other NDEers does offer
solace. You have a ready and sympathetic crowd with some experience in the challenges to come. At the IANDS conference I
attended, it was a strange thing to walk down the hall and make eye
contact with strangers, exchanging mutual feelings of recognition.
This led to the most interesting "breakout" sessions in the hotel
and conference area lobbies, restaurant tables and booths, even
corners of the bookstore. People shared very personal details of
their lives, intimating to me everyone is working on the integration
phase, wondering how they're doing and what is coming next.

The level we go to Inside defines the new version of ourselves
that we become and the new sense of connection to certain people
over others, within the NDE or any other community. You return as
a different person with different values. You are attracted to different
people and different things for a variety of reasons. You're also
avoidant of many people and things that were once familiar. The
old things fall away. It is a ruthless process but no one is to blame.

Events which shocked you before your NDE are barely notice-
able now. Your judgmental values give way to genuine compassion.
You can parse thoughts and truths with a finer razor and make new
distinctions than you did before. Sometimes your feelings flood in
with the force of a tidal wave and you say something before you
can catch yourself. It might not be socially polite, but it's the truth
as you see it. Or you say nothing at all. Underlying all this is an

increasing honesty; you can't delude yourself anymore. Having once looked in the mirror of truth, whose reflected image could not be filtered through the ego, you can never see things as you did before. Where you might have wished you'd remembered a snappy comeback when confronted by a deserving jerk, in letting go of the need to be the smartest kid in the room you become the wisest *adult*. People do feel it.

It's in this time you realize what a solitary path you walk. It doesn't have to be lonely but you're kidding yourself if you don't see you have been separated from pretty much everyone else.

How do you stay connected to the heart of the experience? Since it now gives life meaning and you feel connected to it, how do you commune? Many say meditate, many say pray, many say just live life, and some say try and forget it ever happened.

Some of my best mental ruminations bear fruit when I am out for a drive with God and the In Between. Entire conversations emerge. If I don't somehow make note of them right then, I later have no idea what was said. I record audio notes on my phone. Without that, much has been left in the moment. That's OK, as I'm now sure the truth is always near.

Here are some of the thoughts and ideas that emerged in my meditation drives through the Connecticut countryside:

JUDGMENT

---

As you wake up into the new, post-NDE you, you find yourself in a continuous re-discovery of self. In these changes, you can consider all implications more deeply. In short, is what was true yesterday still true for you today?

Buckminster Fuller said that if you are doing the right thing, the Universe will support you (not *the* Universe), and usually just in the nick of time. Many times, in my past, help came at the last minute. Help probably came in a million other less-obvious ways in which I was oblivious as well.

With time and repetition, I gained some experience in seeing or sensing the patterns in which I was helped, and with that came less worry and more faith, even when waiting past the point of no return. It became a game in fact, using the last few minutes in which everything was about to turn to disaster, to look more deeply into ... everything.... for recognizable patterns of the emerging help coming. I realized also that waiting until the last minute was God's calling card.

As I approached the one-year mark after my NDE, I was shown how Interconnectedness works through my relationships. Watch the people and the relationships; take nothing personally.

*Watch how God works through people.* I realized God works through us and we have no idea what's going on. Think about that. Everyone is on his or her own journey, and most of us walk with the illusion we're in control at least for a few minutes of our day. The fact God can work through anyone to do what needs doing intrigues. This concept was reinforced recently by Tricia Barker, who had an NDE in the OR and saw the power of angels working directly through the hands of surgeons on her broken body. What is the person feeling right then? Do they feel good, purposeful, confused or nothing at all? Seeing this as it happens, I'm now in a place to recognize it and ask in a way natural to the conversation.

Take someone who worries about the net-total each day of virtue and sin. Now imagine that one day God used you to help someone. During that moment, are you without sin? Could those God-inspired actions ever color so outside the lines as to be, as the world sees them, unlawful? After all, to go from being a law-abiding citizen to a criminal is sometimes no greater a leap than the whimsy of a politician's pen. Just ask those who participated in the Underground Railroad.

In the bigger picture, since God can work through anyone at any time, where is the question of eternal damnation? Is this a simple choice of us asking Him to fill our days not with the fruits of our desires or the purposes of our lives, but with the meaning of His? If so, where does judgment come in?

*"Otherwise you fall into contempt of your neighbor, if you judge his evil will towards you, instead of My will acting in him."*
Catherine of Siena, The Dialogue of
Saint Catherine of Siena 1370

FREE WILL

How many times have you heard people wonder if there is free will or fate? To what extent has the illusion of free will contributed to our suffering versus making choices with a sense of being beholden to another person or higher purpose? Yet for the play we call Life to move forward, this illusion seems necessary to the drama.

The first thought I had is that there is both free will and fate. Fate is what happens to you throughout the day over which you have no control; suddenly losing your job, winning the lottery, a loved one distractedly says something dismissive and hurtful, or having or causing a traffic accident. We may have a minor role of awareness or take some small action, but we have no say over the outcome. But to the unexpected loss of a job, we can choose to become despondent or feel liberated; to the impossible winning of the lottery we can choose to spend, save or donate; to the loved one who doesn't realize they hurt our feelings, we can respond with offense or forgiveness. A traffic accident shows us as either an instrument of the cause or a party to the effect shows us a myriad number of choices on how to respond and therefore define our roles in the range of possibilities.

This is where another possibility between free will and fate exists, when God takes over and directs our actions, without us knowing. As much as for any other reason, this can occur in answer to our prayers. I mention this a few paragraphs above. God may help us by working through others, and He may also answer our prayers by moving us to act in unexpected and new ways.

We may have no idea why we're suddenly inspired to go left when we'd usually go right, or thoughtfully listen when we'd normally fill the silence with our own comforting noise. In those moments, God's Will works through us. I'm curious to meditate more on this, because this is where living within His Will, while not being necessarily being conscious of It, come together. When I was aware, I was usually required to act very quickly without time to think about the opportunity presented me.

As I've seen, when all else fails, God designs situations unique to us where there are no other choices than for events to unfold in an unavoidable way. The only way to atone for our past is to change the course toward our future through our choices and decisions. The future, as a set of probabilities, is more important than our past, frozen without change. It is in the Now we choose, collapsing one of those waves of possible futures into a single moment of reality we call the present. In the end, God creates the Universe because He wills it into existence, moment by moment.

## STRUGGLING WITH RELATIONSHIPS

Anyone who has looked at the after-effects of NDEs may have seen the statistic that 65%-78% of experiencers eventually go through a divorce. Those who have an NDE return transformed in ways that constantly surprise them and those around them. The way they think, speak and react to the familiar and the new has changed according to the changes in their values. A loss of fear of death, less materialism, and feeling generally more love and less judgment are some of the changes noticed, often causing their friends and family to struggle with retaining their sense of closeness. If your values change, it represents an ambiguity to any personal relationship, and ambiguities are *never* welcome. They represent a threat with a big question mark...usually at the end of "what about me?."

In terms of after-care, there are counselors and therapists who have experience helping those dealing with their NDEs. If you go to a marriage counselor, make *triple*-sure the therapist recognizes the validity of your experience. Otherwise, your partner, who keeps judging you according to your past and wondering where their spouse is and wanting that person back, will make more sense to the therapist than you do.

Depending on their specific discipline, therapists have their filters to listen and observe you through. A Freudian will see your behaviors and explanations in one way; a Gestalt therapist, another. But if the therapist thinks you are full of crap with all the talk about this "NDE-stuff", you can expect to be criticized for being self-absorbed, understandable as every day you realize you are reacting to the world differently and wondering, "what's next?".

You will also be accused of hiding behind some other crisis in your life, such as middle-age, in order to disguise your change of habits or some dissatisfaction with the relationship in question. Let me say now, if your therapist can't accept the validity of your experience, **DO NOT GO**. It may cause unnecessary and irreparable damage to your already shaky marriage.

As you begin this counseling journey, some inconvenient truths soon surface:

1. The Truth will set you free. But first it will make you miserable.

2. Just because you are put on the path to Enlightenment doesn't mean you are Enlightened. You still have to do the work. Your advantage is you now know the direction to go.

3. The path to Enlightenment isn't for everyone and it's definitely not for all couples. What if one person is now uncontrollably sucked into it and the other, while a good person, isn't ready for such a journey, even as a patient companion? This brings into question, "did God break my marriage?"

4. In the end, everyone must decide what they can handle or leave accordingly. If they stay together, while there will be tense times, there is so much to be said for hanging in there, whether due to vows or a love that goes deeper.

5. Not that this is usually the problem, but it's important to remember that there is no sin in being tempted. Both Jesus and Buddha were.

6. If your non-NDE partner leaves or kicks you out, you can hardly blame them. They signed on for one type of marriage and now you're giving them another. In a strange way, you're not honoring your end of the bargain whether the things in contention were ever voiced or not. You represented a certain type of person defined by shared or tolerable hopes, dreams, fears and desires. Now you are no longer that person and your spouse has to decide if he or she can handle the change.

Think of it like this: if you died, is your spouse saying they would not remarry the type of person you are now? Because that *is* what has happened. The old you is dead and not coming back. Were they done with the old you? Are they able to transition from the old paradigm to a new set of hopes and dreams? Are they OK being married to a stranger who looks just like you? Will your acquiescence toward death be misunderstood as a lackadaisical attachment to a life with your spouse? Does he or she want more of a fighter?

7. This can impact your relationship with your parents, siblings, and children. Next are your friends and professional relationships. It's wise to remember "no one builds a statue to you in your own village." Unless your illness or accident leaves a visible mark on you, then you're no different than before in everyone's eyes. We don't need to cover the disparaging things they will say if they don't believe you had an NDE but expect, "why you?" or "just because you had this experience doesn't make you smarter/wiser/holier than before." They don't want to accept you may now be more than you were, because it means you are more than they are and they are uncomfortable having you in their life. This is where you realize we see life here through the filters we want and on the other side, through the filters we need.

Every time you open your mouth and voice something different than you would have said before, usually marked by greater patience, love or insight, may be met with irritation now. Finally, you may feel they don't want you to say anything at all; This is the world kicking you out. You're going to need some new friends. You may need to look for others who have re-defined themselves in ways like you and that's why NDEers form their own groups, meetings and workshops. Once you feel a connection that touches the core of your change, it's hard to go back to the world. You start to see what many people call *love* is nothing more than attachment.

8. You may need to play-act to keep your head low and your changes as unnoticeable as possible while you figure things out. First, don't talk about your NDE or dawning awareness to anyone whom you know it irritates. As much as you may want to tell your husband or wife about an experience that is now bigger than your marriage to them, I'm telling you now that it's better to wait. Do you want to risk having them shoot down this precious experience? If you're not ready to deal with that or the eventually of a divorce, then the path of misery lies before you. By all means, walk upon it if you'd like.

None of these "truths" are particularly comforting, I know. But as one Zen mystic said, "hearing the Truth should disturb us." The only way I know to deal with truths, a technique of culling what I *want* to be true from what is actually true, is to simply Let Go. See what happens next.

Though the NDE-experiencer struggles with relationships, they very much want to have them. This can be complicated by a more open heart to everyone, where men see women now as mothers, sisters and daughters and women see men as fathers, brothers and sons. Yet where mixed-sex friendships are concerned, most in the world are still struggling with that particular mote in their eye. "It must be about sex," and though it may be for some, it isn't for all and it is less so with those who have died.

Celebrating life doesn't always take place below the belt. But for spouses who have not had such a transformative experience and were attracted to their husband or wife in part because of physical need, it is a mystery they can't fathom, a truth they can't believe, and a hurt they internalize to themselves or project upon the other.

9. This points to another truth of an NDE experience; the ability to see many more shades of gray between the two polarities of right and wrong, truth and lies. The higher life is rarely binary.

Just as religion is a simplified version of Spirituality, most people need simplistic black and white terms just to *survive* life.

Keep putting one foot in front of the other, intuiting your path. It's not important to know the future, only to see the beauty of how everything fits together. In the end, our stories don't begin here, nor do they end here. We're all just passing through.

My last thought on therapy is that despite my frustration with it, I try and avoid beating therapists up too much, as we're trying to understand something that's not totally understandable. If the therapist hasn't had an NDE, how can we expect them to do more than intellectually accept the possibility that we have? I wonder if there are some perspectives they could borrow from studies in PTSD, Multiple Personality Disorders, and other Depersonalizing experiences to help NDE'ers better understand how they changed and more importantly: the *process* of the changes. The story of our experiences from a process-perspective *is* a somewhat depersonalizing, objectifying path so perhaps it would be easier to identify the signposts behind us, next to us, and those around the next corner in integrating the experience.

While feeling separated from the masses and recognizing the aloneness, it is possible for the ego to creep in as a defense from the perceived or real shunning; one is therefore "Chosen". Funny thing is, this could be true. But to feed the ego with it isn't the right path, though ego, in terms of identifying self on a good day and trying to incorporate a new sense of self on a bad day, does play its role.

It's funny how self-absorbing a depersonalizing experience can be.

LOVE

On a recent Martin Luther King Day, I felt inspired to do a little research.

When we see chest-beating brutes defending ruthless actions in personal or professional relationships, many people refer to Darwin and Natural Selection, citing "survival of the fittest". Some of these references are popularly misquoted from "Origin of Species", but the point pretty much boils down to, "kill or be killed". Evidence abounds of a fear-based culture believing that there isn't enough to go around.

- Did you know that in Darwin's "The Descent of Man", he mentions "survival of the fittest" only twice and love ninety-five times?
- He writes of selfishness 12 times, and 92 times of moral sensitivity.
- Of competition 9 times, but 24 times of mutuality and mutual aid.
- And of something else our world is in sore need of, mind and brain - he writes 200 times.

It has been conservatively estimated that 5% of the world has had a Near-Death Experience. With a global population of 7.7 billion people in 2019, that's 385 million. The 2019 population for the USA is 329 million. India has four times that and China, five.

I'm not sure how many people are poor, obese, suffering from one disease or another, but to think there is the common thread of a deeply transformative experience running through 60 million more people than live in America makes me consider what it is to be a member of this seriously-sized population.

Could it be NDE experiencers form one of the greatest single majorities on earth? Now, here is a bombshell question: What if this is the Second Coming? Not with the arrival of one person in the world, but by the spiritual emergence within those who have spiritually transformative experiences? It would be no less paradigm-busting than the Original Arrival. And it would be for *everyone*.

So what is love? First, let's start with what it is not.

It is not attachment, especially attachment to things that are here today and gone tomorrow. That's suffering.

For instance, things only have life for us for as long as we give them our attention.

When we were children, our attention gave life to one toy we had to have no matter what and when we got it, sometimes it was wonderful and sometimes it met less than our expectations. *Either way*, before long it was under our bed, gathering dust and forgotten. It was the same as we grew into adulthood, picking up and putting down boys' symbols of power and sex and for many girls, symbols of beauty and love. Forgive me if you think I've made a gross generalization, but I certainly speak to the eons of generations that have come before, and I am not sure about everyone today. In that case, if no boy is interested in power or sex or girl in beauty or love, then I indeed stand corrected.

You can test this. It's especially easy if you are single and on a dating website. Find someone you think attractive (remember the word "glamour" *means* "illusion") and reach out. Engage them in a conversation. Early on, ask them if they are having trouble finding interested parties who can turn their projectors off- who can stop projecting every fantasy about a potential date or mate they've had since childhood in order to see the other person *behind* the projection.

This one question may gain you some points as well; it's a good practice. Try to not see other people in terms of your projections which, when summed up, amount to "what can do you for me?" See them as they truly are, warts and all. Try asking yourself the question, "how do I need to be loved?" instead of "where is The One?".

There are people who don't feel loved unless they feel the boundaries of relationships on a constant basis. There are those who feel love should make you free. I imagine anyone who understands people remain together not because of a ring, a piece of paper or even a vow but because they simply want to, also understands marriage takes place in the heart before the wedding as much as divorce takes place in the heart before separation. People are with who they want to be because they simply want to be with that person, for whatever reason.

Love is about Letting Go. It is said that if you let something go and it comes back to you, then it is yours. That's also true if it never leaves.

If you have an NDE and find yourself at odds with your spouse in a session with a marriage therapist, you are within your rights to counter any issues cited as pre-NDE and are no longer present, if indeed true. The bad habits of the pre-NDE'ers are dead, because *now* contains the person your spouse is *now*; there is no going back, only building anew.

Furthermore, if this discussion applies to you, it puts the finest point on it I can imagine. As with most people, if your marriage vows clearly state, "until death do us part," what happens when one of you dies? No matter that you return? In such a case, wouldn't your covenant be broken? If you stay together, it is now simply because you are free to choose to.

## CAUSALITY

I wonder how something so personal as my life, down to the most microscopic granularity, could be represented as something as impersonal as a machine. The machine-like appearance of my future, the egg housing with the gears inside, may be my natural way of seeing things and the way something would need to appear to call out to my intuition in understanding how it works. I don't know if you show up like a key and the right lock presents itself. Perhaps some hand behind the scene has the ability to know and give you what you need. I'm sure whatever you need one second from now is there in the In Between.

Why does it matter? It doesn't get more personal than looking at every second of one's life with personal yet unclear choices in their super-positioned probable states with clear meanings and varying degrees of impersonal pain. It's all about probabilities and choices. Was the gear itself the choice or the result? The cause or the effect? Interconnectedness says they are one. Therefore, it is an illusion some people get away with things -- an unpunished thief, the anonymous insult, a prowling predator -- but in the In Between, you will feel the impact of things you've long forgotten and have yet to consider. As one mystic said, "to breathe is a sin", as we kill millions of organisms in the air with every breath we take. It simply cannot be helped. The trick is to find why suffering is woven into our living here on earth and how we can burn that karma off daily. If not, it's more than we can handle as one lump sum. The best answer I've got is daily meditation- connect to the Divine and burn off the things that attach to you here.

The Egg-shaped machine looked impersonal because it is built upon Law. The Law of Karma powering the Wheel of Dharma: Sowing and Reaping, Giving and Taking, Choices and Consequences. The cosmic equivalent of Chutes & Ladders. Set it in motion and it has no choice but to cycle accordingly until what fueled it is spent, whether a rocket, gravity or human desire.

However, as we ask a jury or judge for mercy, we ask for God's Grace. No one can say it is his or her due. It is the power of our sincerity to change, to be willing to struggle, to hate being in our miserable situation that gives our voices the power needed to reach God. When during our Soul's Midnight, we call out His Name. If our heart is ready, He calls out *our* name. On that day, you're going Home. It might take a while, as God frees the fine and beautiful scarf of the soul from its eons of imprisonment in the thorn bush of the world, all the more entangled by the whipping winds of desire.

As choice and consequence are interconnected, we make it *easier* for God to help us when we make good choices, rather than bad ones from which we need rescue. God works within the law He himself created and so do we. Therefore, let our prayers not be a constant and petulant whining to be saved from conditions of our own making. We must come to that place of acquiescence and accept God's Will. If the only time we have for God is when we are miserable, what type of heaven will we have? We define our realities both in this world and in the next; here by what we want, there by what we need. If we aim high, we shoot high. If we aim low, we hit low. We win the associated prize. There are heavens (other planes of existence) that are imperfect and shorter lived than others, existing only as long as the person visiting them is there.

RELIGION & SPIRITUALITY

---

Religion more or less translates as "to bind back." It makes you wonder how you can bind back to something if you didn't have an existence in this life before birth. One thing is for certain, God made man and man made religion. God may have instructed people how to live, but nowhere did He dictate all the pomp and ceremony that define religion. He didn't say priests couldn't marry. He didn't say burn witches at the stake. He didn't declare war on unbelievers. He did say to love your neighbor as yourself. How did religion become so many times twisted away from God? Perhaps the human mind shouldn't be told what it shalt not do, only what it shalt do. With people, it's better to not complain about what you don't have and simply ask for what you want. One is whining and the other provides actionable intelligence.

Religion is left behind when you step over to the other side. While over there, you may see Jesus or someone you think is Jesus; I can't be sure and I'll be the last to tell someone they *didn't* see Him. Somewhere between here and there, you realize people don't burn in hell because of how they relate to God. They aren't punished for what people think they would or should be judged. People damn themselves.

Once, an Indian mystic meditated so well he would leave his body and travel the heavenly realms. One day he meditated and went to a place we would very much describe as hell. He stood on top of tall cliffs and looked out across a vast plain below. Across this plain were scattered small fires stretching to the horizon. He realized someone was standing next to him and looked over to see Vishnu, also looking out over the plain below. The man said, "what are all these fires?" Vishnu answered, "those are the individual souls in torment." The man returned his gaze to the fires and considered their incredible number. "I see that you must be very busy". Vishnu asked what he meant. The man replied, "well, all these fires need tending." Vishnu responded, "you don't understand. I do nothing. They bring the fires themselves."

This is consistent with stories from NDE accounts that say we create our own realities there. When people say they've seen a familiar holy figure or a long dead loved one, have they? Or were those who are there to help colored in by our projecting something familiar or expected upon them? All of us know people who aren't happy unless they are miserable about something; they're tending their fires. Others are content and happy no matter what. Why wouldn't we project our familiar manifest traits? characteristics? upon the latent or un-manifest unknown when on the other side?

A good test is how people deal with mysteries and ambiguities. If ambiguities scare them, it reveals much about their inner worlds. If another person welcomes them as one of the great mysteries of the universe, then this too tells us about who they are. Some people can't wait to travel the world and embrace the unknown and others are terrified of it, certain they will be killed by anything foreign.

People face life this way. They face death this way. In both cases, their expectations may be fully met. By the Grace of God, they may have a surprise and be lifted out of their darkness, allowing for people who don't share their values to live in peace, to marry into their families, to teach them in schools and to one day become the closest of friends. Not all of your closest associations have to be like you, share all of your values or worship your same God. If God doesn't turn their food to dirt and their water to mud, if he doesn't keep the sun from shining on them, why should anyone else? The energy, time and opportunities we waste in judgement drain us dry, make us bitter and age us before our time. The remedy is to simply let go. Take it off your shoulders, put it on the ground and walk away. Don't look back.

Where people are sincere, I love their religions. It binds them back to God and it binds them to each other through the strength of social connection. A lot of wonderful memories are made in places of worship. For those who miss a day in church, temple, or mosque, if they feel badly about not going and miss being with their friends who went, it's better than the friends who went but think about how much fun their missing friend must be having. *However* we get to God, whatever we do to be mindful of God, is commendable. Of course, I'm not talking when people kill each other in the name of fundamentalism. Again, that's all left at the door when you step through to the Great Beyond.

After my NDE, I slowed my praying, as most prayers are a lack of willingness to accept our realities. some with outcomes we ourselves created. If we are to pray, let it because our will folds into God's.

It's been said religion is the tip of a finger pointing to the moon. Spirituality is the moon to which the finger points. It's not as important where you begin as where you end and it's a long journey. Best get started now.

ANSWERS AND UNDERSTANDING

---

God did not break any rules in saving me from unfortunate choices, but I believe He bent them. Upon my return, I felt humbled in the same way you feel in utter defeat. I equated it to looking in a mythological mirror of truth, one without the benefit of ego-filters; I was forced to see me as I truly am. Being stripped to nothing gave me the ability to remove bad decisions from my future, as dispassionately as the machine itself was built to run. There wasn't the usual NDE-related embrace of unconditional love but the opportunity granted for this task is Grace beyond Words. This was the reality of Matthew 6:13, to "remove temptation and deliver me from evil." It is worth considering that God put me in a position to answer my own prayer. There is no free lunch, but we are given the responsibility and opportunity to work with God and therefore save ourselves. Ultimately, it is not by faith or effort, but by simply letting go. If a child constantly socializes with adults, it eventually acts more adult-like and naturally sees life and its choices from a more adult perspective. This is why one-on-one teaching and mentorship is superlative in educating children; educate means, "to draw forth."

As it is natural to ask about what I learned about the future, I only remember two events in my future and they are related to my family. As I was told in the In Between, knowing future events wasn't important in my case. Only the removing of those that caused pain and seeing how that absence was accommodated by the Universe. If I knew which stocks to buy, which ones to sell, which people are faithful and which will stab me in the back, then I would live a lopsided life, as would most of us. It's being hurt that helps us work through our own evolution, and as the pain taught me in the In Between, pain also helps evolve those who cause it. God still wants us to go through discovery and experimentation rather than rote memorization of moral codes or by knowing the future. If we were born perfect or fully informed, what would be the point?

Think about it this way. No one escapes one tragedy or another. How would it help you to know all of them, their time and place, beforehand? Would you spend your entire life running scared from the events of one day to the next? Also, if you were a loving parent, tying your child's shoes after packing lunch for school, could you give them a hug and kiss as they walk out to the school bus stop, knowing on that day a car would jump the curb and kill them? Therefore, most of us don't want to know the future; we can't handle it. If we did, we would be put in the unfortunate position of trying to hold on to life here, or if we let go and realized bad things happen, we'd be called a psychopath. It's not an easy road, is it?

To give life meaning and our lives purpose, there must be a balance between chasing the right questions and meaning. Embrace that, and the filters you see the world through change. Choices you discarded before suddenly pop into focus. Ones you chased lose their luster.

Because we tend to spend all our lives coloring in people and places according to our hopes and fears, even to the point of revising history, I wonder if the same process, reinforced over a lifetime, applies on the other side. On the one hand, people who have NDEs report seeing loved ones who have passed over and welcome them to a new, beautiful experience. On the other hand, especially with children, if they see what they think is an angel or God, they may ask, "is that your true form?" and there might be a shaft of dazzling light. I wonder if the spirits there to help us over are not our deceased grandparents but are happy nonetheless to let us cast them in whatever role we need to come to grips we're not in Kansas anymore.

Returning from the other side, many of us find ourselves divorced from things that defined our past. That person died and remains dead. The noise we loved now pains us as cacophony. The sights which thrilled us now over-saturate us. Attraction for the food we indulged in and intoxicating drink are gone. We eat less, we drink simply, we seek less stress and realize the past is dust. As old attachments fall away to the point we forget about them, new ones don't have any staying power and run their courses quickly.

Emptying out, any thought that fills us, fills us more, increasing the power of how we direct that thought, whether by fear or desire. In becoming empty, we see how the after-effects of NDEs increase. Not the product of emotion but the flow from the In Between to here. The emptier we are, the greater the connection between the two states. When doing this with another NDE-realized soul, the effects amplify. If 5% of the world has had an NDE, that's 46 million more people than live in the USA. Imagine if that population of 375 million people all emptied themselves at once to become conduits connecting The In Between to here. What do you think would happen?

The power of that single intention brings me to my next thought, **single mindedness** versus **perpetual distraction**.

A fire hose with leaks along its length reduces the water pressure at the end of the hose. Have enough leaks and you can't put out the fire. Plug all the holes in the hose and the water will focus its power through the end. In the Tao Teh Ching, it says that we should be like water, humble and seeking the lowest place. Yet nothing can live without it and its power can carve canyons. This is the power of our attention. Within one lifetime, the Wright brothers delivered powered flight and sixty-six years later, Neil Armstrong, Buzz Aldrin and Mike Collins took us to the moon.

Attention also gives life to things. When we were children, an advertised toy we saw on TV and that our friends were excited to have, became important to us. If we found it under our Christmas tree or in the pile of birthday presents, we were initially happy to play. Several months later, the prized possession gathered dust, forgotten under the bed. It's that way with everything else in this world. The new car, the new job, the new girlfriend or boyfriend. At some point, our attention shifts and that which we have gone to war over is forgotten.

Practicing being present is an exercise in removing distraction from our minds and other demands on our attention. That comes with a new way of processing information and perceiving the world around you.

BEING PRESENT

---

Being present is akin to becoming a blank slate or a still reflective pond. If you look at something, it exists. When you look away, it doesn't.

Some NDEs don't result in bringing back psychic powers. Maybe the experiencers come back with nothing more than a Connection. With their change in perspective, they may bring back wisdom. The average person is interested in what you saw and the acquisition of any psychic abilities. But fewer ask, "what did you learn? How are you wiser?"

The In Between spoke to me to pay attention to my relationships because everything is interconnected. At the same time, I felt an aspect to walking with God that's incredibly solitary. There are things you can't share because people will think you're crazy or because the experience is so personal.

Imagine the difference between sitting in a theater with the entertained, distracted masses and going solo on an expedition. At some point, if you love adventure movies, wouldn't it be natural to get on a plane or ship and go have an adventure? When you come home, people will want to know what you saw and hold the souvenirs you brought back. Some will ask what you learned about others. A few will ask what you learned about yourself.

Earlier, I mentioned the challenge of being present in the In Between versus being present here on earth. There, you process information non-linearly, taking in the whole enchilada in a moment. Trying to apply a non-linear perception to a linear world that deals with time has surprising drawbacks. When present, I can't process a movie as its scenes are sequentially delivered in linear time. It is like an amnesiac watching a movie one frame at a time, forgetting what had just happened and unable to predict the frame to come. This is a hazard to living here- when you are present, you don't take in information as usual and you don't process it normally either; you perceive patterns instead of steps and intuit their relationships and purpose all at once. It can be a challenge to living here and another challenge to those who are closest to you and don't understand. This is what I meant by having to go find your Truth in places the World says, "there be Dragons".

Answers and Understanding are both important, but we are neither the answer nor the understanding. We have become the question; that's why we search. Once we are present, we're the whole thing, the Question, the Answer and the Understanding In Between.

When you are present, time stops and you are in Observer mode. While in this mode, you may notice the worldly part of you working through something but the real you passively watches, without forethought, afterthought or judgment. You are also at peace.

This is where the comedy kicks in, the "downside" of Being Present.

**Memory and Attention are affected.** You can't have had such a stamp placed upon you without serious change. For instance:

1.  Full On Attention narrows the focus of reality to near zero and expands the "now" towards infinity. This increases your tendency toward single-mindedness. That gives your thoughts more power. That increases the times you see them manifesting, and you feel that this begins to define synchronicities. Manifested thought makes synchronicities. To that point, not long ago I was thinking how my work isn't very fulfilling and it doesn't feed my soul. Within a week, I had a previous customer express the desire to hire me as a CIO and reorganize their company. At the same time, I was asked to produce a 10-part documentary special, and I haven't touched a film camera in twenty-five years or been in the field for fifteen.

2.  Being Present means you can't process information in linear time. You can't watch a movie. If you're giving a talk you must have prepared notes; you can't play strategy games on your phone in the middle of the night because you can't remember anything or plan anything. In studying the difference in processing information linearly and non-linearly, some of my other NDE understandings have stronger footing.

## SYNCHRONICITY

One thing is for sure, after an NDE, synchronicities come more often. It's the way God and the universe encourage you to take the next step on the right path.

In January 2018, I went to a business networking dinner and sat at a table of eight people. As everyone was going around the table sharing their backgrounds, true to form, I couldn't help myself and talked about my work and hobbies and then slid right into the In Between. Those who were spiritually inclined asked questions and those who are not just stared at their plates and used their forks to push their food around. I was surprised by the general interest, the excellent questions and the overall sense that those who were interested understood my story. One especially interested man, Nestor Rodriguez, reached out to me with more questions and we have stayed in touch, both looking forward to the day we're brought together for some professional endeavor. A few weeks after the dinner, he emailed me the photo below, which was near his office in New York but only recently had noticed it.

*Comparison of the In Between egg and the one standing near the corner of Avenue of the Americas (6th Ave.) and W. 54th Street, by Pratt Institute architecture professor Haresh Lalvani*

A couple of weeks after that I was invited to a luncheon in New York and the topic for discussion was "Kindness Unedited". I find the topic and the location of this event interesting for two reasons:

1.  When I left the In Between, I was told to pay attention to my relationships, and everything is interconnected. "Kindness" as a reason to get people together for a meal fits.
2.  The location of the luncheon is exactly where the egg-shaped artwork in the photograph sits. Out of the entirety of New York, I find that interesting.

During the luncheon, several people got up to talk. They spoke more of the kindness they had received and been humbled by rather than the kindness their elevated positions in society had bestowed.

## THE IMPOSSIBLE NOW

One concept from the In Between was the Impossible Now. It was "impossible" because of its incredibly short duration, and its infinite width. By design and how we fit within it, you are forced to be Present, as In That Moment present. Inside it, there is no past and no future but an infinite expanse across universes. This is why it's easy to get lost within it and experience difficulty even thinking or talking. In speech or thought or writing, you normally think of the next thing to say as you get one statement out. In the Impossible Now you forget the next thing you would think of saying as soon as it flashes into your mind. You are simultaneously in an observer mode even as you speak. I sometimes read a day later what I write while in there and wonder who wrote it, as I have no memory of doing so. As I have said elsewhere, the In Between isn't a place you go to or come from. It is simply a place you are.

I sense also an association of this impossible thin-ness of the present with walking a razor's edge of focus. When we focus down to that quantum level of infinite shortness of Now between the future and the past, the width of a razor blade becomes wide enough to walk upon.

I've spoken before about the importance of Understanding over Answers. That is because Understanding reveals Meaning and Answers reveal Purpose. Both are important, but purpose can take you only so far. It may be event-specific and at most, lifetime-specific.

When I removed gears representing bad choices in my future, I have said I wasn't guided by some moral compass or recitations from holy scriptures. I was guided by the pain of the choices I'd made, and those of the choices my current path would present for me and choices likely to be made. As I removed them, I have no idea what they were, nor did I need to. They hurt me, so I got rid of them. It was that simple. The need to know what they were was replaced by the understanding that they were bad for me. It doesn't mean I won't still make wrong choices, but there is less chance now they will be bad ones.

If you still think answers are more important than understanding, I'd ask you to consider how that worked out for Adam and Eve, when they traded the fruit of understanding and meaning in the Garden of Eden for answers and purpose in the world, born of the Tree of Knowledge.

Back in late May of 2018, I went to visit my mother in North Carolina to help her with the final paperwork preparing for her eventual move to an assisted living facility. During the few days I was there, we accomplished everything needed.

On my way home, I noticed I felt differently about my connection to life. This was the marked change I felt since my plane crash, how I felt about the In Between and my connection to this world.

I would characterize it as feeling lighter in spirit, happier. I also felt more engaged in the world and less moment-to-moment mindful of the In Between in the same connected way as before. That bothered me, as I never want to lose that connection to the Beyond the NDE gave me.

Yet I thought further and asked, "isn't helping my mother the correct response to the In Between's telling me to 'pay attention to your relationships', as it tossed me back to earth?" If following Orders resulted in differences of feeling about that which commanded me, then it must represent not just a change of state, but an *evolving* state, sanctioned by That giving the orders.

It was also around this time I gave my first presentation of my experience to a group, a local IANDS group in Farmington, CT. I worked on my PowerPoint slides and updated my notes every few days. I flew back from Charlotte for a couple of nights for this express purpose. On July 9th, 2018, I couldn't have asked for a more beautiful day or more welcoming crowd. As I spoke and read aloud the conversation with the In Between, I felt it fill the room. At the end, people mentioned they had felt it. To me, that made the talk a success.

A few days later, I was contemplating how Einstein's equation $E = mc^2$ essentially states that as we (as matter) approach the speed of light, our mass approaches infinity, distance approaches zero and so does time. Meaning, if/when we transition from matter to light, we are everywhere there is to be and in an instant. This is one of the reasons I feel I was in a single moment in the In Between, while my body aged a week here.

In my talk, I referenced Max Planck, the "father" of quantum physics, born *before the Civil War*. He believed in a non-personal God, much like I experienced Him in the In Between. Impersonal as in He is our natural state. It's not like our arms wake up happy to see us, we simply know what to do with them the minute we realize we have them. Kind of like that. Planck Time, where quantum phenomena are observed, is in the Impossible Now of the In Between, measured as 10 to the -44 seconds, or a hundred millionth of a trillionth of a trillionth of a trillionth of 1 second.

I referenced in an earlier mention of how there are at least two entangled particles, one at the beginning of time, and the other at the end of time. Across an infinitude of space and an impossible expanse of time, whatever happens to one immediately happens to the other. The interconnectedness of all things. Therefore, within the "In Between" those two particles of immediate causality, everything else - The Present/The Impossible Now/Planck Time - exists. I was shown how the Impossible Now is impossible because of how thin (in duration) it is, yet unimaginably wide, across universes. In that single moment of the In Between, it makes sense that I was light, not only because my body was not there, but because the egg-shaped machine of my life was at a standstill. Either it is because where I was (as light) no time passes (it doesn't for light), or I was moving so fast (as light) that it's like working on your car engine while it is running, because, at the speed of light, you could take the whole thing apart and put it back together again between piston strokes. Either way, I understand. In a state of that stillness, a stillness where we aren't collapsing one of an infinite number of probability waves into a present moment, we become light.

The more Still we are, in that Impossible Now between what comes next and what is turning to dust, the more we reside in a state of pure Potential and come closer to this powerfully unmanifest aspect, the closer we are to the Highest (Unmanifest), God. In that suspended unexpressed state of all and equal probabilities, we are every place there is to be and in every time there is to be.

We are One with all there is.

## STILLNESS AND LETTING GO

On the field of battle, when a Samurai draws his sword and throws his scabbard away, it is because he will never need it again. Little does it matter whether we win or lose, at least as the world sees it. Fighting with courage and heart and total abandon, we use everything we have. We embrace death because we are greater than death. This is only possible when we Let Go.

What if we do that when faced with what seems an insurmountable challenge?

What if we live that way every single moment?

Some things are so huge that it's more a matter of heart than body.

Do you believe this surfer for a moment thinks he can fail? You must be Present to pull this off.

*One of the largest waves ever surfed. Nazaré, Portugal*

Spiritual studies and quantum physics state that every moment is infinite with probabilities, our conscious decisions continually collapsing one of them into our present reality. All of these probabilities have a reality in which each is chosen, with every moment spinning off into an infinite number of directions. Wherever you choose to go has its own timeline and your original one would remain intact and your history unaltered.

And yet, if we're all one soul, interconnected, and living out each of the infinite number of realities at the same time...doesn't this speak to our divine infinitude? This only hints at what "children of God" means.

It's at our still point of meditation where we become present, that we realize we're within the nexus of all probabilities.

> *"To the mind which becomes still, the entire universe will surrender".*
> Lao Tzu, Tao Teh Ching

> *"Be still and know that I am God"*
> Psalm 46:10

The word "still" is translated from the Hebrew meaning to "Let Go". Elsewhere in my story is mentioned *The Art of Letting Go*:

> *"All the force of Will you will ever need is found in the art of Letting Go. Always live Life in celebration of the individual spirit. For no one, no thing, can stand before the brilliance of a truly naked soul."*

JOY OR ACQUIESCENCE?

---

Many are the NDE tales of feeling Joy and Unconditional Love. Many holy texts in the East praise the emotional state of acquiescence. Certainly, it seems transcendent to rise above the duality of the pursuit joy or avoidance of sorrow, to have moved beyond both.

*"Content with whatever gain comes of its own accord, and free from
envy, they are beyond the dualities of life. Being equipoised in success
and failure, they are not bound by their actions, even while performing
all kinds of activities..."*

Bhagavad Gita: Chapter 4, Verse 22

What is the emotional state we should go for? With all the stories of
beautiful scenery, joy beyond words, and love beyond measure, in
comparison, my experience didn't fit in very well. In fact, I would
say my experience was emotionally vacant. I simply accepted what
came. I was in what looked like Purgatory and I appeared to be
alone, but I accepted it as natural and was unafraid or feeling in
need of comfort. I knew I was there for a purpose and the need
to stay on task was paramount; hence the words, "you're not here
to feel good."

Bringing these ideas and feelings back to this world is prob-
lematic. It's amazing how much social lubrication is made of
everyone agreeing on how to feel about things. People want you to
feel like they do as a form of social cohesion and that's how they
bond. Logic tells you what's correct but emotions tell you what's
important. Which one contributes the most to our attachment here?
Logic ties to ego and intellectual pride but emotion confuses many
primal cues with lofty ideals. How much does what we mistake
for love pull us to the bosom or strong shoulders of the world?
How much does what we mistake for selfless service pull us to a
self-serving patriarchal role deciding for our neighbor what is best
for him? One of my mentors said one time, "make people feel and
they will love you. Make them think and they will hate you." Both
politicians and preachers have taken this to heart.

Regardless, when you don't get excited, insulted, chase joy
and dodge sorrow like everyone else around you, those in your
immediate group will question whether your values are the same,

whether you place the same importance on your work, your play, your family and your God as they do. Nothing is worse than having to fake enthusiasm.

To drive home what my gut tells me about the higher ideal of acquiescence, here is a story that helps:

There was a king who heard of a holy man, a carpenter, in a village within his kingdom. He sent for his high priest and asked that he travel to the village and check the carpenter out. The priest dressed in normal clothing and traveled by normal means to the village, without the trappings of his office. In his disguise, he found the carpenter and stopped to talk to him while he worked. The priest noticed that the carpenter was building a casket. They make small talk and after a while, the priest was wondering where the 'holy' part was. The man just seemed to be like anyone else. Suddenly, a neighbor ran into the shop, announcing to the carpenter that his only son had just fallen off the roof and died. The carpenter then nailed the last nail and looked up, not at the neighbor but at the disguised priest and said, "I know."

Obviously, the carpenter was spiritually developed, and knew more than most of us. But in this, where was his joy? He had Peace and Acceptance. The concept of joy is irrelevant. Who of us can walk this path? But it has the hallmarks of the type of development we should all pursue, though some would think it sociopathology.

I'm not saying it isn't nice to feel joy. I am saying I believe the goal is to feel it when it is there and let it go when it subsides. Don't avoid sorrow when it comes to call either. Just embrace it, be sad for the reasons needed, then also let that go. Don't let either define you.

Another challenge to the status quo is this: Is not the state of equanimity, beyond joy and sorrow, that allows for a full experience of pleasure and pain without the normal attachment and resistance, the better choice?

In contrast to many NDEs, I felt no joy in the In Between but rather an intense sense of purpose, like I was/am on a mission. I guess removing bad choices from my future could be happiness but the exercise was not joyful, per se.

Mission and purpose are part of the quantum level hair-splitting I do now.

*"Be who God meant you to be and you will set the world on fire."*
St. Catherine of Siena, Letter from St Catherine
to Stefano di Corrado Maconi 1347-1380

Catherine of Siena also referred to what happens in the In Between as the Perdition of the Fires of Love. These are not pleasant places, but they are good places. These are the fires where the noblest are forged.

Finally, though a somewhat colorless place without mirth, I find it interesting that when I feel my presence in the In Between, it radiates through me and attracts people. I believe this is because in the In Between interconnectedness is more apparent than it is here and when in touch with it there, that radiation...radiates here. Even though it doesn't look warm and fuzzy, returning from that place you can't help but bring some of its radiation, to which *everything* strongly responds.

As strange a place as the In Between looks, people show an interest in its depiction. One time I ordered a large print of it on canvas and the Director of Marketing for the company called me to talk about it.

## HONESTY

No lies are allowed in the In Between. After having been there, it's harder to be less than completely honest here too. Thinking about it, we generally tell ourselves lies to get through life and sometimes, just today. The intensity of the purpose-driven version of me and the "Nowness" of my time in the In Between made for no dreams, no illusions, no lies. There was no memory of the past or anyone here. There was no fear, no joy, just an extreme laser-like focus.

I had a clear feeling when I was in the In Between of this enforced honesty. I characterized it initially by saying being there was like looking in a mirror of truth, one that strips away the ego and lies we tell ourselves in order to look into the mirrors in our homes and not wretch. We are not perfect; we haven't gotten to where we are by being perfect. Many made less than ideal choices. What happens when you arrive in a place where self-delusion simply can't occur? I wonder if this is the reason I felt sick to my stomach my entire time there. That being in the In Between stretched my limits to the point of pain.

When I was given the opportunity to reach forward into my future and feel the sector gears representing choices, some made me feel more nauseous and added to the pain I felt. An unthinking reflex made me pull them from within the construct of my life and throw them away. After a week removing bad choices from my future using a non-God-pointing compass and only pain to embrace and live with those probabilities, I realized I felt less sick, enough to say I could now live with the changes. That's when I was sent back.

It was genius I couldn't see the choices I needed to discard. As I reached up into the egg giving birth from the future to the present, I could only go by feel. If I could have seen the gear that showed me winning the Powerball but made me feel horrible because I'd become a complete ass by doing so, I'd have been tempted to keep that event in my future, promising to not become worse than I already was. I was only given the blindness of feeling as my guide. This is what was meant when the In Between said to me: *"If those with choices make poor use of them, then offering fewer possibilities could be called mercy."* I pulled, nonstop, 24/7, for a solid week. I also heard this:

> *"Eliminating bad choices doesn't mean you won't make wrong ones. You won't know they are wrong until after they pass. Since right and wrong are variables over which you have no control, the answers to what comes tomorrow are a waste. Better is understanding the beauty of how everything fits and re-fits together."*
>
> *The In Between*

## FAMILIAR FACES

It is mostly reported that what we see and experience in a Near-Death Experience is presented in ways we can make meaning of; each is tailored to our state of development and understanding.

As the "place" most people report going to is pleasant and comforting (not all are), I wonder if those who appear as loved ones, those who've already died and welcome us there, are actually spirits whose job it is to help us transition? Spirits who could care less how we color them in?

If we color the place with things comforting and familiar, why not color in who meet us as well?

*Each according to his or her nature*: Is that the way of the In Between? If we need the comforting faces and embraces of our favorite grandparents or pets, then are there helping spirits, happy for us to color them in accordingly? The In Between seems to know everything about us and presenting loved ones may simply speak to how readable souls there are, while for the newly arrived, their eyes have yet to adjust

There are many accounts where the temporarily dead (NDEer) asked if the person's form was their real form. Sometimes the answer comes with a transition into an orb of light.

Many people think when their spouse dies, they will meet them on the Other Side. Why should that be? I guess this is how many deal with their grief, and I'd not one to deny them that. Are people called away from this world to simply hang out over there with nothing better to do? Especially with regard to their own Development, they simply wait for the surviving spouse to die? What if the spouse left behind remarries? What if the remarried spouse again becomes a widow or widower? Who meets them when they die? In all this, people seem to forget that in their marriage vows, they are agreeing to be husband and wife only for as long as they both shall live and until death parts them.

It's been widely stated that in an NDE, we "get what we need" to learn something, to get our life back on the rails, to realize what's important, or any number of other reasons.

It's also been stated things there take on a shape meaningful to us, as part of getting what we need out of the experience.

In that the places we go or see, the sounds we hear, are tailor-made to our current level of understanding, could it be the "loved ones" who welcome us and help situate us there or steer us back here are not long lost loved ones but kindly spirits whose job is nothing more than help us adjust to our new reality? Do we just color them in with faces we trust in order to get through the magnitude of the initial shock? If we color in this objective reality ("bigger than just us") with the subjective familiar (trees, meadows, flowers, how God and angels look to us and so on) in order to understand what we're supposed to understand, then why not in the In Between as well? I've also wondered this because so many people console themselves with a deceased spouse waiting for them on the other side. What if they are not? What if "until Death do us part" means just that?

I'm not wanting to rain on anyone's parade and no matter what I consider, I know the truth will be self-evident There. But if I want to see things as they really are, and to the extent I can stand, it's worth asking the question now.

## SOUL GROUPS AND CONTRACTS

Some of the groups I follow ask big questions about physical life here and the life of the spirit. Many ask about purpose and meaning in life. For the most part, purpose gives rise to meaning, based on the perception of patterns that emerge by simply living and observing life.

One perspective says we travel in soul groups, agreeing to "contracts" and "rules of engagement" prior to every incarnation. The love of your life in the last go-round will be your professional nemesis next time and your kids will be your parents and so on. I understand this is supposed to round out our understanding of the human experience. I have actually heard this type of discussion.

But it begs this question: Here you are talking to your "soul group" in a transcendent condition between lives about how screwed up you're going to make each other's lives in your next incarnation. To me, this is a pathology, not a path to Enlightenment. Otherwise, why would we need Salvation in any form? Just keep hitting the Reboot button over and over. The issue is this: What good are these lessons if we forget them with each birth and change of circumstances?

You can't "escape" the wheel of suffering from up there. The work must begin here. Since I believe we are incarnated more times than we have numbers for,, there is a flaw in this perception. Doing the same thing over and over, replaying different roles in the play of life on earth with the same similarly entrapped souls bound to this reality (can you say that? I am trying to find a different word beyond "earth"), is a wretched condition, even if you are at the top of the heap with your own television show and product line and attending sycophants.

For me, the purpose in life is getting out of this cycle. A cat licks a whetstone because it thinks the blood it tastes is from the stone, not its own tongue. That's an inconvenient truth for sure.

I am hearing people talk about soul groups and contracts. I assume the concept is groups of souls form a type of collective and time their reincarnation cycles to come again and again into each other's lives, playing different roles each time; parent/child, spouse/lover, boss/worker, tyrant/victim, or mortal enemies. I'm answering the question, "Why do we have to return here at all?" I say, "To learn to Love."

Taking this idea a step further, imagine two or more souls are in a more enlightened state between lives, they can see and understand things hard if not impossible to appreciate here from this mortal perspective. Bottom line, when "There," we are "More" than we are "here". If the above paragraph is correct, when in a more enlightened condition, we have sane conversations with members of our beloved soul group about coming back into the world and into each other's lives, and sometimes not as those who love each other, but as people who may try to kill each other with great intensity. One could even be the serial killer. Max this thought out as far as you can.

I have an issue with this for the following reasons:

1 - With a more enlightened sense of self, we communicate in normal tones about leaving that state to return to the squalor of the world, put on a dying meat sack of a body, take an amnesia pill and a stupid pill too, and start killing each other....all to teach each other about love....when we're already in a place where subtleties and the power of love is experienced in a way not possible on earth.

2 - Just as we've seen how gifts can pass from one life to another, with five-year-old Mozarts and ten-year-old Einsteins, so too can damage; hurts pass from one lifetime to another, preventing a soul from blossoming, from living a full life and realizing "love." We, in our more enlightened state, agreed to do this to each other?

3 - As I wrestle with an analogy to further state the absurdity of the concept, I imagine playing with a child and her dolls. We move the dolls around, using different voices, and we plan out our day with the dolls going together here and there. Then imagine I start tearing the dolls up, ripping them apart. Once they have been destroyed and their parts thrown all over the place, I look at the terrorized child and say, "this was the lesson about Love we agreed to before we were born. You meditate on this now and have a nice day." You tell me, does this make any sense in any world or on any plane of creation? (great!)

4 – I can't believe there is any explanation that convinces me we terrorize each other to teach love.

WHAT IS YOUR BEST VERSION?

Have you ever asked, "what is the best version of myself?"

It's natural to reflect back to the happiest or most productive times of our lives, either personally - with friends and family during holidays or some momentous occasion, or professionally - achieving some goal that resulted in recognition, a promotion and/or salary increase.

What if the best version of yourself wasn't when everything was going right, but when everything was going to hell and you were getting your ass kicked?

Why are the heroes in stories not those who were born with a silver spoon in their mouths, but those who were knocked down over and over again, sometimes only picking themselves up from the dust because if they didn't, it's right there they would starve? Is it because all of us know adversity of one form or another and so this is how we identify with the hero's journey? Or do we look up to them because we admire their strength and determination to not fail? Do we love the hero for whom success comes easy or the one who holds back nothing, about to lose so much there's nothing left to hold onto?

When this life is done and we look back on it, will we love the version of ourselves that was happy with and defined by relationships, or when we went alone to fight our most fearsome dragons? Even if we don't win, will we evaluate our performance by that score, or by what we found within us that gave us the courage to try?

In the end, which is better? What will people remember us for? Is this not the stuff of ballads?

Consider then, getting the crap kicked out of us is the opportunity to see what we're made of, our character, our love. That this is our finest moment. That this is the best version of ourselves.

If these are our finest moments, are we willing to return to the struggle on earth to continue the work of our creation and evolution?

ATONEMENT

---

The past is dust. You can try to atone but only by making better choices in the present, as the future unfolds its infinite possibilities into the Now. Using one's desire to do better, to think better and to be better will filter the choices we make to a fewer set of probabilities, and blind us to other, unfortunate ones. We may still make wrong decisions, but they will not be the same bad ones grounded in the seven deadly vices.

As part of my consideration on Atonement, I ran it through the lens of the Soul Contracts within our "Tribe" as I did above.

Imagine that, between lives, we are off stage and reviewing the scripts of lives when we will live together on earth so we are able to move through the ups and downs we cause each other in a somewhat objective manner.

Now imagine we are all born, grow, and come together to play out our roles as defined by our scripts. Imagine one or more of the lives lived are the stuff of nightmares and evening news reports.

One day all these people will pass away and regroup between lives once more.

In past life regressions, sometimes people who revisit those lives understand their predispositions and fears as a result of past trauma experienced in those lives; a fear of water due to drowning, a fear of burning to death, a fear of guns, perhaps even a fear of relationships. In that these traumatic events left an imprint on these souls, scars carried from life to life, my original point was made regarding "how does this teach us about love?" Especially if we do these things to each other not as payback or karma, but "just because"?

Now here's the kicker: Even if the cosmic setup is such that if I hurt you in this life then you can hurt me in the next life to keep this weird cosmic balance, *is* there really balance? Let's say you shoot me in this life as I try to protect my family, dying knowing you will kill them too and that I was unable to fulfill my duty as a husband, father and protector, then how exactly does my killing you in the next life make me feel better about this original hurt? I am saying it's not just our physical bodies that are hurt, but parts of ourselves that survive death, that reincarnate, and even create our future lives. These hurts become part of us. It is an asinine concept to think we're all good now because we have just lived two lives in which we killed each other and now everything is all right. My question makes me aware that trauma continues life after life, , taking a break in the higher planes *does not*, despite its higher understanding and broader view of The Big Picture, bring healing. It sets the stage for the next suffering.

All this back and forth of reincarnating to what? "Get it right?" is a waste. The need to return again and again for whatever reason is attachment to living on this plane and therefore subject to the joys and sorrows that can only be experienced here. It's like the Uncle Remus story of the Tar Baby. Don't touch it, because you can't untouch it. You're stuck to it.

Where does this line of thought lead us? What *is* the atonement for hurt so deep it goes across universes and epochs? Total and absolute detachment to any sense of self, a drop returning to the ocean and being re-absorbed into oblivion. To become so present time ceases to exist, including past and future. To live every moment on that razor's edge is like driving a major highway for you but for almost everyone else, it's a high mountain round. In the Bible, it says God will Himself wipe away the tears. Not that retribution or atonement will. You can't force yourself out of your victim's hurt any more than you can stop feeling guilty because you caused it all. While we come to this understanding, we just need to live life helping each other and putting no new stones in anyone's path.

This recalls how the zealots wanted Jesus to kick out the Romans from Israel. If you believe in His divinity, certainly He could have. When asked about healing all the sick and dying, He said sickness and death have always been here and always would be. That is what this world is. So no, He wasn't going to kick the Romans out because it wouldn't fix anything. His role was to point the way out. When the house is on fire, you don't stop to paint it and you don't stop to pack your belongings. You focus on getting out.

GRAY

---

Detachment implies an unbiased disposition toward one outcome over another. You can see processes and flows from further away than close up. As you fall into the beauty of the processes, seeing them flow, carrying us all- action or inaction - to wherever we're meant to go, it's as if you intuit the cosmic mathematics within each flow, just as an illiterate caveman could run to catch a ball tossed to him without being conscious of the calculus, charting the ball's parabolic trajectory accounting for wind deflection, speed and so on. In the end, you find yourself drawn to do the right thing, not because of some reward or even because it makes you feel good, but because the "math" in the situation calls for it. You aren't looking for a connection to the common or greater or even a private Good, you're just following the math equation and solving for "x", and the correct answer is the one that *is* good. Then it is on to the next flow, the next math problem.

I notice a process emerging where? In everything?. It's like my NDE, in pulling me out of line and cutting off the pipeline of how desires, fears, hopes, and dreams fuel my attachment for being here. Since my NDE, if I go out and try and do any of the things I enjoyed or was otherwise drawn to before, it is with less attachment, less pleasure and in some cases, less pain. It's not that I'm numb, it's more like I'm emptier.

The world I went to was gray, not full of color and this world becomes grayer every day. With the pipeline running dry, everything I do here feels hollow, like I'm running on fumes. Imagine you go to a movie and enjoy it a little bit less than the time before. Restless in your seat, you look for something to engage your attention and so you watch from a technical point of view: studying the camera angles, the timing and choice of the music. Now imagine the same for every other aspect of life. Relationships feed you less and less. Thank heavens it's not a clean break but one that while accelerated, is paced to what you can just stand. The desire for financial stability, and the worry over instability, grip you less over time.

Sex has nothing to do with love and fades away as the associated need (lust?) turns to vapor. Even your favorite foods have less taste as you realize the body is nothing more than a machine that needs fuel. Love, in the majority of cases, feels like nothing more than the fulfillment of projected desires upon the world around us.

With the transactions of "what can you do for me" established in work, romance, families, religious beliefs and being negotiated every single moment of every day, our subconscious watches and waits to react to any momentary dip in the negotiated deal. And an NDE represents perhaps the greatest survivable dip of all, as those "closest" to you who don't have the transcendental experience ask, "Where did *you* go? I want my friend-spouse-coworker back". And there you are, standing with a blank look on your face, at first unknowing of the Change, scratching your head and wondering what they mean by asking, "how do they know?" People can tell when you're engaged beyond the obvious things or subtleties of nuance, voice inflection, choice of words and body language. You can feel it in just their touch, whether they are present or distant.

It's like the gray world of the In Between *infected* me, as I become grayer every day. I am pretty sure the reason the world looked like it did was so that I wouldn't be distracted by rainbows and unicorns and would focus on my purpose. As within, so without, they say. In as much as I didn't ask for it, the answer appears to be coming. I can only continue to put one foot in front of the other and see where it takes me. Remove all else, and you hear Silence. Adjust your eyes to the dark, and you can see the smallest hint of light. I've seen my way across sand dunes in Africa, hundreds of miles from anyone, with nothing more than starlight. As each photon reaches the end of its millions of years of travel from space longing for a brief touch of our faces turned upwards to the night, we *meet*. That briefest moment *is* the Present. The past is dust and the future is many possibilities rolled up into one just waiting for us to choose.

## DESIRELESSNESS

While in the In Between, I was inside a single moment. In a place where time stands still, you don't change. You stop identifying with the parts of you that change. You're aware of conscious observation, processing information non-linearly. You understand by getting the whole enchilada and unfolding its patterns and processes which say everything about it.

A computer can download a 2-hour movie as 1s and 0s in a few seconds with the story all there, its nuance, the hero's journey, the formula of what makes a good script and the potential within all those binary numbers to change people's lives and win international awards. But we need a media player to translate that 2-minute download into a 2-hour movie that we can understand. Now imagine absorbing all that at once as receiving the entire experience. That's because where there is no time, there is only now. Remember that at the beginning of time and at its end, there are two entangled particles that affect each other, meaning that between them there is no past and future, only the present. And truly, that's the only period of time in which we can live and act.

Being in such a state stamps an indelible impression into you and you'll see an after effect upon returning that allows you to sit motionless, staring at a wall for hours. Your sense of passing time changes. All your other reference points in life will also be affected. You'll feel fewer desires because they are associated with change and stimulation, things you feel less associated with now in communing with the sublime.

Like so many other things worthy of attainment, whether Acquiescence or Desirelessness, it's not about girding your loins for battle and wrestling with the devil, your ego, your lower nature or anything else; it's about letting go.

What *is* the Art if Letting Go? It's sitting in that timeless place, not holding onto anything, letting anything that comes pass around and through you. Not chasing anything. Not running away from anything. Just observing. Not reacting. None of it is you. All of these flows have always been here, things flowing through the multiverse that are sometimes chosen as tools toward achieving ends written into incarnated souls' destinies or desires. That's all they are, impersonal tools in the trade of incarnating to experience whatever plane or reality we're focused on at that moment.

Here, you are within all the probability waves, in a state of possibilities, ready and poised to choose, to collapse whatever probability waves are needed to move in a desired direction. You can stay in a state of potential, which feels like a very powerful place because it is. Your will is free, until it acts. Then it will surf the causal wave it sets in motion and that is where karma begins, as much reflecting the intention as the action. If you can act without desire or intention, you can act without generating fresh karma. That is the middle path. But to know if your actions are generating new karma or paying off old karma, you have to see the causal relationships you are putting into motion when you collapse the probability waves into a moment of physicality which then reverberate off into their many directions. I know that's a lot to swallow at once. It is with intention that we do anything. An opportunity presents itself to us in life, and from this, our desires wake up and want to explore it; a job opportunity, a potential date/spouse, a possible answer to a big question, and so on. Once the fire is kindled within us, we begin moving heaven and earth to get to the goal the opportunity represents. That intention is what creates new karma, planting seeds that will grow into things we need to account for, whether good or bad. If we can't account for them in this life, then we will in another. And this is what forms the circles of the world, the links in the chains, either of iron or gold, which bind us here.

The higher planes are sublime, and this physical plane is known for its intensity. It's a drug. We like loud music, spicy foods, strong drink, wild sex, power over others, wealth beyond measure, fame and glory and to not get caught and punished when we commit crimes. Until we can perceive, then prefer, the hidden over the intense, how can we deepen to and stay within these planes? Why would we want to?

David Byrne was right, "Heaven. Heaven is a place. A place where nothing. Nothing ever happens…".

Chapter Ten:

# Easter Sunday & Christmas

---

If you think of how only the three traditional cups of wine were passed among the group in the Last Supper; the fourth Jesus said He would forgo until He was within the Kingdom of Heaven. It was on the cross someone placed a sponge of soured wine to His lips. In taking it, this became His fourth cup of wine and then He said, "It is finished". It's meaningful this "cup" of wine was bitter and marked His conclusion here.

The path of the spirit is not for the weak of heart. And in the end, more than courage, Heart is what it's all about.

In reflection of my NDE, I have realized how hopes and dreams backfill into the present, impregnating the choices before us with their reflections. Seeing which choices we can make increases the probability of bringing us to our desires, and we choose accordingly. But what happens if a transcendental event cuts the roots of attachment in a way that also withers those attachments? What happens when you realize you *have* no hopes and dreams? Things that colored your day; how the sky looked, how your relationships were defined, including your place in the universe, and how they have given you purpose, all come to a sudden and immediate end. You realize the few attachments you *have* left are no longer fed by the past or the future; every desire, every joy and pain you enjoyed or suffered yesterday or tomorrow are now running on fumes. Feeling empty is another commonly reported feeling after an NDE. Not only do the old hallmarks now seem empty of joy, but the things that hurt you also have less power to make you miserable.

To become empty of desires means you perceive all possible outcomes at any moment with equanimity and less bias than before. Yet this stage of spiritual change can be discomfiting as you wonder if this growing emptiness is a sign of things to come, or if something else will fill it? I've heard it both ways, but it seems the more detached Eastern approach embraces total emptiness of the target, while the West preaches we will be filled with joy. However, I'm concerned that to be filled with anything that has a polar opposite is *not* perfect balance.

As I become emptier as a result of the depersonalization experienced on the other side, I have less and less in common with this place or its fears and worries, much less its hopes and dreams. Yet I feel self- contained, so it's not a given that a solitary path is a lonely one, but there is definitely a feeling of having been removed from the crowd.

CHRISTMAS

As news got out of my satellite-videophone gizmo, Microsoft heard of me and flew me out to Redmond, WA for a visit. At this time in the 1990s, many companies were experimenting with content-rich internet sites. Microsoft had its own travel and adventure site, called *Mungo Park* after the Scottish explorer and edited by Richard Bangs from Mountain Travel Sobek. They wanted to put a team together to retrace the journey of the Magi, and they were interested in my production background in wild areas and, of course, my system. With it, we could travel in harsh, remote conditions and stay in touch by telephone, over the internet or directly with live video.

We began in Iran, went through Syria, Jordan and Israel, broadcasting live on the Mungo Park website with video from

Manger Square on Christmas Eve. Why did we begin in Iran? Because in Marco Polo's book *The Travels of Marco Polo the Venetian*, references to the Magi state two of them came from an area in Iran noted by a Zoroastrian temple fortress called Kala' Atishparastan (Cala Ataperistan), or "The Castle of the Fire Worshippers". I include this small expedition in appreciation for the mysticism of Christmas, eclipsed by increased commercialism. That these people who followed a very different path and who lived so far away knew from their internal development of the birth of Jesus, *has* to honor those for all time who are of different faiths but walk toward God. We should celebrate this fact by inviting them and visiting them, during each other's religious holidays to share in the social bonding and friendship. There should be no either/or of the monkey mind of duality.

The following photos are of this place. We asked some of the locals if they'd seen any other Westerners rummaging around and one elderly man acknowledged a French team visited the site in the 1930s. Truly, it was a rather untouched place as things go these day; pottery shards were strewn everywhere and even a coin or two. If many tourists visited, it would have been picked clean, with trash left behind as well.

In the first photo, you can see the seven tall arches with straight sides in the outer wall. This was the representation of Ahura-Mazda (God) in the middle with his six archangels around him, three per side. The Zoroastrians were commonly referred to as "the Fire Worshippers" as they kept a fire perpetually burning in the temple and didn't allow it to go out.

*Cala Ataperistan, the Zoroastrian temple fortress from where it is believed two of the Magi came from. The seven recessed rows with the arched tops are representative of Ahura Mazda (God) in the center and three archangels standing to either side.*

*The architecture melts into the landscape.*

*Adrian climbing up the steep trail to the top.*

*Author Paul Roberts and I in one of the fortress chambers*

*Herringbone pattern of ancient mud brick.*

*Across a very dry and vast plain, looking out from the*
*walls of Cala Ataperistan toward Afghanistan.*

*One small pottery shard I brought back, holding a votive*
*candle and surrounded by the Three Kings*

Chapter Eleven:

# Doing This Yourself

My experience in the In Between removed future choices that are a detriment to my spiritual development.

When we sit in meditation here, we pick a quiet place free from distraction. Similarly, the In Between was a place in ruins, where I couldn't be distracted. A post-apocalyptic city offering no reason to explore it, no other people, no other visible life, no way off the building I was on top of. In fact, such a place is analogous to a blank canvas, evoking the symbology I needed to best interpret and act upon the experience. For someone else, the In Between might have appeared as a beautiful garden in need of weeding.

My depersonalization was another aspect of removing distractions to stay on task and on target. I had no memory and therefore no attachment to my life here or to anything else. I had no attachment to my individual sense of self. To the greatest extent I experienced and remember, I would say even my ego was not apparent. Although I was in a scary looking place, I was not afraid in the least, hence by my intuition I understood why the construct looked the way it did. Stripped as bare as possible to the core of being with no attachments, I was as neutral, as gray, as possible. That includes emotionally as well. Be as neutral, as gray, as you can.

This neutrality set the stage to see in the clearest way possible the work that lay before me. Without attachment, without desire, without fear, I could see the choices in my future and feel no desire to keep one or avoid another, based on anything other than the pain touching them would give me.

To ensure my detachment held, I couldn't see all the bad choices I could make. I had to reach high up within the egg to feel around for them. When I touched a bad one, I felt immediate sickness in my stomach and pulled the gear out to throw it away. Within this statement, as disassociated as I was from everything when I was inside, it's interesting I still didn't see most of these bad decisions. I wasn't allowed to. Perhaps that's because their temptation was still that strong. The In Between said it wasn't important I see or know of these instances.

In the split second there, I was incapable of processing information in linear time. That is the other reason I was told not to worry about the actual experiences I was removing but to *feel* the choices and the pain each probability inherently offered. In the In Between, we might not be able to process information in a linear fashion, but we can understand pain, even if within Planck Time of $10^{-13}$ seconds.

Humbling an experience as this was, I have wondered how it could be translated into a practice that others could also experience and take benefit. It's not another path to "Prosperity Consciousness" or a heretofore unknown Law of Attraction. More likely, it is a statement that you already have everything you need and you always have. All you need is to remove conflicts with your purpose, that which gives your life its meaning. The force of will needed isn't in girding of one's loins for battle with the serpent, but simply taking its weight off your shoulders, putting it on the ground and just walking away. It's the Art of Letting Go.

When we become still, there is no effort to be aware of; you feel all manner of possibilities swirling around you, with you at the nexus, the literal crossroads of decision. Even now, in a fully conscious and engaged state of mind with the world, you can feel in your gut the certainties of the various aspects of life you have set in motion. If anything is at a pause because others are having to make decisions, you can feel that thread out in the cosmos, like a spider's web. If something occurs on that strand of web, its movement causes a vibration that ripples a wave back to you and there is information regarding this possibility wrapped up in that vibration.

Imagine yourself with threads of cosmic spider silk stretching out in every direction to future moments on their way to the present. Some of these strands will represent possibilities of greater, some of lesser, focus and activity; you can feel them with invisible hands and in your gut. With practice and repetition, you can begin to feel the certainties of their coming to fruition. The more accurate your intuition becomes, the less you worry about such outcomes. You may still have desired results, but will you find yourself caught out with no alternatives less and less. If you worked hard on something and even got others who need to be involved excited about it but you're not feeling those little vibrations, you'll find your attention and energies turning to those threads that do communicate distant or future work being, or that will be, done. It's simply so much more apparent as the way things work now that I don't even think about it.

Having already adjusted to that paradigm, I'm still exploring why the change in imagery from spider webs to gears in the In Between. Sometimes changing up your frame of reference is exactly what you need to consider fully what is happening. In this case, more information could be conveyed about the probability of future events by the associated gears varying in clarity and definition as they presented themselves to me. Those less clear and defined are either further out in time or less certain to be chosen or even to eventuate *as* a choice. I can feel things coming into expression, swirling around me all the time. and I like suspending my choices for as long as possible before choosing any for the same reason we extend tension in any experience; the longer we wait until we eat, the tastier the food. The longer we wait until we drink water, the sweeter it is. The longer we wait to return to the embrace of our beloved, the more amazing it is when we do. It magnifies the experience of being Present.

Not rushing choices and waiting as long as you can before you have to choose also allows all the other possibilities to mature a little more as candidates for selection, removal or denial. That increased maturation allows for the arrival of new information that might impact your choice. In practical, worldly terms, it makes sense. As an example, one time I had two opportunities simultaneously present themselves as a result of creating my vacuum and then releasing it in a given direction. This is what is done when you are still, present and understand how you feel. I thought with clarity what I felt was missing in my life, then let it go and sat in emptiness. That is creating the vacuum. The desire or awareness of what is missing is aiming the vacuum.

Within the week, two offers came in that were wonderful but appealed to two different versions of me and my professional background. I believe they were constructed by God to ask me the question of what is important to me. Neither are more right or wrong than the other, just driven somewhat differently.

Nothing can happen if the practitioner can't become still. That means not being too attached to outcomes. You need to take your bow and shoot the arrow because you love shooting at a target. Winning a prize is a totally different thing and distracts you from shooting perfectly. You have to choose between process and content. The process is the formula and the content is the graph you get when you plug in values for $x$ and $y$. Just focus on shooting and the winning or losing will take care of itself. You don't have to see or know every possible choice you can make in the future, but you must *feel* them. You might feel them and yet not know what they are. All you need to know is whether they feel neutral or good or bad. If they feel bad, if they run counter to your values and emotions, let them go. To know which ones are not right for you requires being honest and knowing yourself.

Some unknown propensities of our minds *can't* be known until we are operating at a level in which they surface. A quick look at Maslow's Hierarchy of Needs gives us some useful perspective. Within a pyramid of human experience, Abraham Maslow described several levels representing the evolutional maturity of man. The first level deals with the primal basics of food, water, shelter, procreation, safety. Once those needs are fulfilled, we progress to higher needs and socialization skills. We ponder the world around us beyond the immediate basics and so on, rising higher in the pyramid with ever more evolved needs until we reach the pinnacle, self-actualization. Using this pyramid as a map to navigate our way around the human landscape, it is hard to look at people struggling at the first tier of survival and know which of them will become the puppet masters of the world when they reach a higher tier. Or which one will have an epiphany and come up with a cure for cancer.

In our own lives, in the absence of a map or a compass (moral or otherwise), how do we chart our journey? What is our frame of reference? If we have a compass and sextant and understand the principles of navigation, then we may not have a map, but on each new day of our journey, we can still orient ourselves by calculating our position based on the stars to understand where we are on earth. Some things remain constant in the light of our change. That's why the North Star is important in celestial navigation; it is the Enduring Star and never wavers. Make that which is permanent and unchanging to you, your North Star.

Our instrument of orientation – how we reference our North Star - on the inner journey also helps us understand our relationship to the outer world; the boundaries between what we need and what we desire. There is no right or wrong to it, only how attachment can tangle us up in the experience. With everything we pursue and sometimes win, if we could let them go when they have run their course- wealth and power, our beauty and status, youth and strength, our children and life itself, then we have a better conclusion to the overall experience. I totally understand through our financial and emotional investment this is hard to do. I'm still human.

How do you see your own In Between and its meaningful representations of future choices as possibilities to select and de-select? What are the constants across our different models and what are the variables? What of this exercise is individually specific and what is archetypically universal?

Chapter Twelve:

# Applied Science

Thinking of how a process could be established that presents an actionable plan for others to follow, mirroring my experience, I think there are some subtleties to consider that are specific to one's evolution. Can people handle seeing their own death? If they do see it, can they leave the circumstances alone and let it occur? If they can say yes to all that, what about if they see death for their child? Can they still hold the course? One indicator might be by asking a past life regressionist how his or her patient responded to seeing not just their past lives but past deaths.

It is these parts of our stories that make this path so solitary and *not* for everyone. You either are this or you aren't. There is no part-timing this view of life and the world; it's that heavy duty. I would try and incorporate a series of filters to pull back those not ready. This exercise might not be good for someone with certain psychological issues or who suffers from suicidal tendencies. Let me be clear, do what's necessary to stay alive as long as you can. Take care of yourself and those who depend on you.

I know my experience was about removing gears and choices, so it could be argued, "what's the difference?" My reasons, my intentions weren't to avoid physical death but spiritual harm. Intention is everything. Obviously, attachment too counts for a lot.

What if an NDE heals all of your inner pain and maybe even some of your physical pain. It takes a while to realize it, because of the momentum of attachments to things and relationships from the past that no longer serve you, but you do them out of habit.

The rest of your life allows the associated attachments to simply run dry. Some do so it more quickly, some will take the rest of your lifetime. You begin to detect the process as a pattern, as things fall away, as your taste in food, music, people and even former thoughts of "What God Is" change. Your answers to the same old questions deepen and hold more dimensions of perspective.

Which means that the rest of your life involves understanding why you hang on to the things that limit you rather than just giving them up. Of course, that's part of the lesson: in letting go, you also let go of the need to hurry up. This is God working to free the silk scarf of your soul from the thorn bush of the world, in which it has become tightly entangled over lifetimes. He does so gently (even if it requires an NDE; you could handle it, right?), one thorn at a time, lest He rip the precious scarf.

How can we say we are ready to leave the world, to transcend, to experience something so mind-blowing and transformational that only the direct experience of death can bring understanding, when for a day we can't bear to be apart from our families, our work and our possessions? If someone wants to work out their salvation, then they must be prepared to pay the full measure of devotion to God or Guru. It takes *the willingness* for that to succeed.

How real is this to us? Even if we become forgetful of the Divine, once we are near it we begin to calm down. Like the honeybee who flits from flower to flower until it finds pollen, nectar or honey, then clings to those and won't leave them.

The Lord himself is present in both, friend and foe, and we should not, therefore, mind either the amity of friends or the enmity of enemies. The Lord is the mover in both cases. But this cannot be the view of everyone. Only those who are waking up see it this way. This is the acquiescent main axis within the sine wave of duality- of love and hate.

From my Path, here are some quotations from the book *Spiritual Gems (1965), a collection of letters between a guru and his disciples in the early 20*<sup>th</sup> *century, by Sawan Singh* that feel right to me. Reference to the "Sat Guru" is to the highest realized soul a person can be-someone who is truly one with God, like Jesus, or Buddha.

*162. Many people wish that their relatives and family members would believe in the feet of the Sat Guru. The wish is not bad, but it should be remembered that till the Sat Guru looks mercifully upon anyone, it is very difficult for him to have faith and love. This should be left to the Mauj (Will) of the Sat Guru, for when he so wishes, he will confer faith and love in a moment and take them out of the snares of the world.* This reminds me of His response when I prayed for help with my marriage, *"You will have a wife for as long as I want you to have a wife.*

*163. Disciples of Saints feel no pain at the time of death. Rather, they face it bravely because they have already kept death in mind and have taken part in the affairs of the world only as much as was absolutely necessary. They have already struck at the roots of the world within them. The worldly life of the Satsangis of a Sant is like the short-lived greened of a tree which had been cut down.* No pain, no memory, no PTSD; I felt like I'd already made peace with Death. To a great extent, I had minimized ties with the world. I have spoken of how it feels to have the roots of my attachment cut, and I'm just using up what sap remains in the branches of my attachments until they run dry. The green tree has been cut down, and doesn't realize it is dead yet, but regardless, soon it will.

*182. The blind cannot catch one who sees, but one who sees may permit himself to be caught by whomsoever he chooses.* We recognize the divine that surrounds us only when and where It chooses.

Even if your entire life is spent trying to connect with God or finding the right Guru, that time is chalked up as selfless service and not wasted in pursuit of the goal of spiritual liberation. It's important to remember that we go where our desires and intentions take us, and if we attach ourselves to those desires for which a physical form is required, then to a physical form will we return.

*Paraphrase from 193: When people think that they can reach renunciation only through analytical thinking and reading holy books or going on retreats, they are only deceiving themselves.* Where is the test of the mind and of the philosophy in this? There are always challenges to be faced on the earth plane and when the weather turns from sunny to rainy or even to snow, the sensual allure fades. Today's flattery from the rich and powerful evaporates as they turn and chase the next big thing. Our minds, seduced by this false love in that moment, seek new ways to re-attract their attention, and in so doing, enter dangerous territory in what will be sacrificed to stand again on that temporary pedestal. Only later do those who have sold their souls realize it is too small a space to walk around on, much less live.

On the other hand, *outward* renunciation, efforts at detachment from the outside-in, reading of spiritual books and singing of hymns also does not represent the path of salvation.

Whether you are the police, the victim, or the criminal, it is the same event in the world's machinations that you are getting attached to. The only way out is out. If you have had an NDE, to whatever depth you have gone, you have been shown this.

We need to diminish our desires for the earth plane; whether to do good, or to do bad. Doing good forges golden chains around us and doing bad things forges chains of iron. Even those who enter the world to uphold the righteous and punish the wicked, while upheld as heroes in legends that will last thousands of years, are trapped in the illusion that this world matters to that extent. As if the wrongs they will right haven't been here since we began incarnating into the world nor will remain long after they, the heroes, are forgotten.

This place wasn't created to be perfect and it never will be. We didn't come here to make it perfect. To try and do so is like pouring water into the desert to make a lake. You could pour buckets all day long for your entire life and with your last breath there will still be only sand. The only way out is Out. Letting Go- of the desire to do good, of the desire not to do bad, of even the desire for liberation. You can only do this from the inside out.

You can't feel your way into sincerity of doing all the right things to leave, you have to get to a place where you are already living that life. For instance, everywhere there are videos, podcasts, conferences and books of people who may present their take on things, or that their take is to be embraced as the Flavor of the Day. How do you know of all these gurus, who is the True One?

The answer is easy. You can't. Even if the guru you are considering has passed all the tests you can think of in terms of consistency between their known lifestyle and their message, the only way you can even begin to know is by simply spending time around them. If they know 1-inch or 1-millimeter more than you, how do you know it's only 1-inch and not 1-mile or even 1-light year? When Lao Tzu said a journey of a thousand miles begins with a single step, this is also true if the distance is a thousand days or a thousand lifetimes, through the earth plane or through every plane up to the highest one beyond manifestation.

The only way to get even a hint of whether your teacher is as high as you need is to see if in their company the power of your vices over you decrease. Do you find your predispositions to anger, or pride, or lust, or laziness... have less of a pull on you? Letting go of desires for *any* world is to recognize that if you are not happy when your desires are frustrated, then neither will you be happy when they are fulfilled. Happiness has nothing to do with desire.

Anything that takes you to the peace and quiet of equanimity, when all the world around you is happy or sad, picking up their karmic credits at the Lottery Office or paying off their karmic debts at the Tax Office, remain away from the ups and downs of joy and sorrow and the desire for emotional intensity. As an *inclination*, be on the main axis of equanimity, unmoving up and down- dispassionate to the opportunities to experience intensity for intensity's sake. The ultimate goal is to live here and create the least karma possible- this is where intention and desire play a role in binding us here. As long as we see the world as something to react to, we will react to it, wanting some things and not wanting others. Equanimity and Acquiescence is accepting of either, allowing to come what may. Nothing can come to you or happen to you that is not yours.

Chapter Thirteen:

# Physical Plane

Imagine cruising through one universe or another and looking at our little blue marble. Now imagine asking what it is all about and someone telling you that it is a place you go to experience intensity. Coming from more subtle planes, that may or may not be meaningful to you. More questions about the types of intensity may lead to more answers that have little meaning to a disembodied soul; gender, race, level of sophistication, war, wealth, disease and so on, mean nothing if you don't have a body or much history wearing one, especially on planet earth.

It might be just as easy to come to earth as an illiterate peasant with few options in life as it would be to come into the world as royalty. From up there, one is about as good as another and being you're already "dead", the notion of an early or horrible death may not mean much. Neither would being born into subjugation or poverty. These things, including religion, only have meaning here and are that short-termed. Yet once incarnated, they become important enough that our attachment to having and keeping, or hating and avoiding, them may result in desires and actions which bind us to reincarnating over and over to chase or avoid them again and again. We begin to forget about who we were before we became… "this". Then we have a slight memory at the edge of our awareness of believing we were more than this, more than an aging body and increasingly decrepit mind. Surely the answer to remembering our full spiritual nature is to be found pretty much anywhere other than where we are; on the other side of the planet in rain forests, deserts, mountains or oceans. Yet in traveling to all those places, we realize the answers are not there, but within us, no matter where we are or where we travel. It isn't a matter of journeying to the Truth. It is about Letting Go of everything else. After all, it *is* our attachment that keeps us here.

This is the plane of Intensity. "There" is a more sublime realm. The highest aspect of God is that which is Unmanifest. Here, we view life through the filters we want. When we look in the mirror, we see the best-looking person in the world. When we hear our name, there is no sweeter sound. When someone puts us down, it's *they* who are wrong and misunderstand us, and so on.

## HIGHER PLANES

As we turn our attention toward Heaven, the Sublime, we move from the manifest to the latent. As our senses are also subtle when in the In Between, we can see things as more obvious than we can here on earth. We don't process things in linear time, so we can get the whole enchilada all at once and know its beginning, middle and end right away. This is why we meet the familiar faces of dead loved ones. We need something familiar, some measure of comfort, in order to orient ourselves and begin wrapping our heads around the sudden channel change from earth to the next plane. Since we go to where we are ready to go, I believe the higher we go (or deeper), the more ready we are to let go of all things familiar and just embrace what's there. I think people see grandma and grandpa and maybe even Fluffy the dog because they *need* to; they project out the need for something comforting and familiar and there are souls who will respond and come to help. They could care less who you color them in to be. They can read your soul, saying familiar things to you as "proof" they are real. All they have to do is look at you. Here, things can be hidden. Over there, you are as naked as you can imagine; you have no real body. You can see the life in things and read their history with a glance.

HIGHEST PLANE

The latent is more powerful than the manifest, if nothing more than because it is full of possibilities. A shrug in the latent worlds of the sublime might be an earthquake here on earth, like a human kicking an anthill in the land of the manifest.

Did you know that the electronvolt (eV) is a unit of energy whereas the volt (V) is a unit of electric potential? eV is how much energy *is* delivered. V, the potential, is what *could* be delivered.

Potential is unmanifested, remaining in a latent, yet-to-be-expressed state.

This is said in the opening words of the Tao Teh Ching:

*The Tao that can be told of is not the Absolute Tao;*
*The Names that can be given are not Absolute Names.*
*The Nameless is the origin of Heaven and Earth;*
*The Named is the Mother of All Things.*
*Therefore: Oftentimes, one strips oneself of passion*
*in order to see the Secret of Life;*
*Oftentimes, one regards life with passion, in order to see its manifest results.*
*These two (the Secret and its manifestations) are (in their nature) the same;*
*They are given different names when they become manifest.*
*They may both be called the Cosmic Mystery:*
*Reaching from the Mystery into the Deeper Mystery*
*is the Gate to the Secret of All Life.*

But manifestation is not a bad thing. We were born here for a purpose and that requires discovery through interaction. Most of us go off the rails at some point, leaving whatever state of grace we were born with.

The truth people want is what they want to hear, not what's inconvenient. If an Amazonian Indian says one gender or another

The In Between - A Trip of a Lifetime

for "God", no one will say a word, so why should this be different for anyone else? If the intention is to bridge gaps for just making the effort to communicate, then can't we grant an allowance to others different than ourselves?

Sometimes it's not about what you say, it's what you don't say. And it's not how you say it, but how you don't that says the most of all. Leaving the silence pregnant with meaning allows people to color it in according to their own evolution. Bringing your thought up to the point of a one sentence summary may be more effective by pausing at that point and allowing others to fill it in themselves. Mozart used this to pull people into his music by pausing on a note and the audience completes it in their own minds, emotionally investing in the music.

Just aim the vacuum so your audience is in the right place for the light bulb to go off.

Chapter Fourteen:

# Seeing Life in a New Way:
# Linear versus Non-Linear

## "WHO ROBBED THE BANK?"

---

*Linear thinking* pursues answers through a step by step process that has a Go/NoGo gate at the conclusion of each step deciding whether we move on or go 'round again. Thinking this way lends itself to very binary thinking: things are black or they are white. These types of thinkers may miss seeing an opportunity or reaching a compromise. Some patterns of information remain invisible to them. They are inside-the-box thinkers because part of the process is "defining the problem" which means "defining the box" and then working on it, usually from the inside. What happens to your problem-solving journey if the primary assumptions or procedures break down? This is how most of the world thinks. It is also impossible to think or process information this way when you are Present.

## "WHY DO PEOPLE ROB BANKS?"

---

*Non-linear thinking* brings understanding by promoting thinking and problem-solving which extends in an outward expansion spiral. This provides multiple starting points from which one can study a problem. Such thinkers can walk around the problem and find the way through, rather than trying to solve the surface symptom. Most world problems are caused by other problems stacked on top. Linear thinking keeps the mind sliding on the surface, going around in a circle. Nonlinear thinking goes deeper, spiraling through different perspectives, revealing other aspects of consideration. This is a more evolved way of thinking. It is also more natural to think this way when being Present. Instead of following the breadcrumbs, you can see the loaf.

Your awareness of this emerges when you realize you aren't using your memory to understand things; you don't need a memory to perceive a complex and dynamic pattern moving in front of you. When you are really Present, it's with no memory of the past or anticipation of the future. It's with your intuition.

In fact, the more Present you are, the quieter you are. In being still and knowing that "I am God" you choose the sublime over the intense, the silence over noise, focus over distraction and dualities like joy and pain withdraw into the main axis of the sine wave of emotion; we walk along that axis, not chasing pleasure or avoiding pain, but accepting of either. When we hear someone speak, their words give us answers, but from their nuance, inflection and body language emerge patterns of meaning. We realize that the short or extended silence between their words is filled with equal amounts of information as the choice of words themselves. Add to this their inflections and body language and you have a more complete picture. Even when we chew on it slowly, we discover new layers and depths with each consideration. Moment by moment, we are changing, becoming something else. Part of this transition may be seeing more and more shades of gray between absolutist binary thinking. This is because we are no longer blinded by that which we once thought we were: our desires and our fears. Waking up like this in a sleepwalking world creates definite challenges. Finding others like ourselves who are coping with this transition helps. And the Quieter we are, the more power in the unmanifest potential we see, while the rest of the world celebrates cathartic explosions of attachment and vice.

I believe God could care less about most of the crap we get all twisted up about. How we live our lives says how close we are to

Him. As we walk to Him, He runs to us. If we are intent on doing something others judge as bad, He won't stop us. He will let us see how that path and those choices work out for us. I can imagine Him saying, "when you're done, come back, I'll be right here. I'm not going anywhere." Otherwise, trying to please everyone else, trying to follow many rules which seem arbitrary to you, means you're living someone else's life, not yours.

One more thing I want to share is a home-grown analogy regarding non-linear thinking. Have you ever been in a meditative or dreamlike state and were aware of thinking about something too big to bring back? Upon coming back, it is on the edge of your memory but you can't bring it to the surface. There may even have been emotion associated with it and that can be stronger than the thought itself. My analogy is this: Imagine you are living in a bottle. The neck of the bottle is too narrow to crawl through but you can stretch your arm up through it and into the great Outside. If someone balanced an orange on the opening of the bottle, you would see a small section of the entire orange. In reaching out your arm into the word beyond, you might be able to hold the orange in your hand. Then you can rotate the orange, feeling its weight and texture. You may even bring back its scent on your fingers, but you can't bring the orange back into the bottle and you can't leave the bottle to see the fruit in its entirety. To describe the orange to someone in the bottle with you, there is only your limited process of discovery with which to use insufficient analogies. But if you *could* go outside the bottle, seeing the orange in that one moment would tell you everything. That's the difference between linear thought inside the bottle trying to procedurize the discovery of the orange versus the non-linear understanding and knowing an orange with a single glance, or a moment's taste.

Here is how I've split a few hairs to categorize some things with linear and non-linear information processing:

**Linear Thought**
- Answers
- Purpose
- Content
- Manifest
- Words
- Logic

**Non Linear Thought**
- Understanding
- Meaning
- Process
- Unmanifest
- Symbols
- Vision

I've shared my understanding of how answers give rise to purpose and understanding provides meaning. Answers are usually the fruit of linear, procedural steps with Understanding being a non-linear breakthrough, "A ha!", moment recognizing a pattern through repetitive procedural process. It's the same for Purpose and Meaning: Yet how firm are you in purpose if you aren't clear on the meaning of your purpose-driven actions? A similar relationship exists between content and process, manifest and unmanifest and words and symbols. Not to mention Logic and Vision.

As an example, I am thinking of a physics lecture I once attended. Our professor was discussing how differently a trip taken at relativistic speeds (approaching the speed of light) would look to the traveler and an observer standing still back at the launch pad. Skipping to the end of a high level overview, he wrote Einstein's simple equation, $E = mc^2$. If you plug in values to this equation, you will eventually see that *if* you could propel mass toward the speed of light (186,000 miles per second, in the vacuum of space), from our launch pad position, that mass would appear to increase toward infinity, its time relative to us would appear to contract toward zero and the distance between it and whatever far distant target it is heading to would contract to zero. Which is another way of saying that if you could go the speed of light, you'd be everywhere there was to be instantly and weigh everything there is to weigh. If you hear that and are spiritually inclined, it more than boggles the mind.

If you take it a step further, this also says that for light itself, there is no time. Perhaps this is why we, once we take leave of this mass, our bodies enter realms that have less or no mass and time flows differently. I wonder if each plane we go through as we go further from the physical one has slower passing time, until we get to the still point in which it doesn't pass at all? Having conceptually stated his case, the professor then wanted to drive home the frame of reference aspect of the relativistic travel exercise, how life would look to the traveler and again, to the observer.

To best demonstrate this, he used math. Most of us are familiar with the Cartesian coordinate system that uses x, y and for a $3^{rd}$ dimension, z. There are other types of coordinate systems we can use locate things in space too. In a two-dimensional world, you can use polar coordinates with a companion three-dimensional reference system called spherical coordinates. It makes sense: polar implies movement along a circle and polar coordinates measure position as a function of distance from some reference point and at some angle above or below a reference direction. Just as when you add a third dimension to a circle you have a sphere, it is the same with adding another reference to the polar coordinate system. On earth's surface, you could use the x,y,z method we all know to stage your position in degrees north or south of the equator and then east or west of Greenwich, England (the reference point normally used in terrestrial navigation) with z being your altitude location above sea level. Spherical coordinates would draw several lines from the reference point of the earth's center: one to you, one to the equator's point closest to you and one to Greenwich, UK. Your position would be stated as the distance from earth's center, the angular amount between your line and the one to the equator and again between you and the line to Greenwich. The professor proceeded to use the non-terrestrial polar coordinate system (as we were talking about flying in a rocket) to prove his theorem and it took three big whiteboards and most of the class to do it. He instructed through the entire exercise to make sure we kept up with him. Then he proved his point and we thought that was pretty cool. Then he looked at his watch and said, "now here is how it looks using spherical coordinates". We all thought his watch must have stopped because there was only five minutes left to the class.

He returned to the board and used one small unused area to write three lines in spherical coordinates. Doing so, he had just proven the power of another frame of reference over another. By stepping outside the two-dimensional world of polar coordinates, to the three dimensional world of the spherical, he could say in three lines what it took three whiteboards and an hour to say. I'm not sure what everyone else thought, but to me this said, "power". I am still blown away by the memory and its significance, forty years later.

This appreciation of looking at things from different angles in search of the highest, most comprehensive and fundamental per-spective was further driven home by my NDE. This was the fertile ground for my two columns of categories above. After my NDE, I began splitting hairs to a finer degree, resulting in these dichotomies.

In terms of content versus process, when you go to the movies next, think of how most people go for the content; the movie star, the genre of story, whatever they like. Process is where you would watch the movie from a technical point of view, analysis of the script, the type and timing of the music as a cue to understanding the scene, camera angles, lighting, composition, focus of the lens on the subject, and even subtext as times and so on. You measure the efficacy of all you analyze by the reaction of the audience. You could get so wrapped up in analyzing the film its content becomes secondary in importance. Yet if you do this enough, you just might learn how to make a movie.

By looking at patterns you discover the underlying formulae that things and events use for their birth, duration and expiration. DNA may look like a thing but the information inherent in it translates into a lifelong process of unfolding. You have to disengage from the excitement of the moment to see the patterns operating beneath. There are styles of speech meant to whip a crowd up into a frenzy, whether by preachers or politicians, and these are usually full of emotional triggers rather than logical ones. Once you realize that, it is harder to be manipulated by the speaker's objectives.

Manifest and Unmanifest. In many religions and schools of philosophy, this distinction is made. There may even be a changing percentage between the two, depending on where on the continuum where your frame of reference is. The higher planes are called the sublime and the lower planes, including the earth, are the manifest, defined by their intensity. Our attention is drawn to one or the other, the excitement of a loud party, adrenaline-driven sports, attractive people we want to connect with, wealth, power, and so on. Things which by their definition are desires made manifest and intensity measured on the cover of grocery store tabloids and social media "likes". It's a merry-go-round and eventually the rider tires and wants to get off. The excitement becomes repetitive. Once you see it enough and the formulas that drive it, what comes next is less of a surprise and eventually, predictable to the point of boredom.

This is where the statement, "the Truth will set you free, but first it will make you miserable" takes effect.

Just because you see the shallowness and predictability of the world doesn't mean your eyes are yet attuned to the more subtle worlds beyond this one. Until then, you may be drawn in preparation to books that take your thoughts in this direction and new friends who are also loosening their grip upon the world. Eventually the time will come when the richest foods, strongest wine and beautiful forms will simply not hold your attention like they used to. As we think, so we become.

As you come to appreciate the subtle over the intense, seeing the invisible threads pull things in and out of viewable existence, your taste for food and appetite for excitement and titillation follow. You *become* sublime yourself. Returning to our books on mysticism and the higher planes, as we begin to experience these more subtle worlds, we begin to appreciate our spiritual growth is woven into a path that takes us from places of greater manifestation to those of lesser, or finer, manifestation. The Tao Teh Ching says the Formless gives rise to the formed and the Primordial was before that which came into the duality of yin and yang. John Milton, the brilliant 17th-century English poet and philosopher. suggested the highest form of God is that which is unmanifest. We begin to sense the power of potential.

I sense that this hairsplitting continues into the powerful difference between words and symbols. When you sit down to a lecture, you can imagine there are people in the audience who may know the subject so well that they can predict every sentence the speaker will say. For them, those who came to hear something new, the hour-long lecture may be painful, waiting for the speaker to arrive at every point they already know. But when presented with a symbol instead of words, each person sees and experiences it in accordance with his or her own background and inclinations.

The people who already know the subject are not slowed down in their intellectual digestion of symbols.

In this way, to each, their own. Think about it. Dreams are more symbolic than literal. It's not often that you will have a conversation with someone when dreaming as their mere presence suggests something to you. Then perhaps their actions, or yours. If you dream that you are taking a college test for which you are unprepared and also are sitting in class taking it with no clothing on, the message of being caught unawares and unprepared needs no words to drive it home. If you fly in a dream, you may enjoy the ecstasy of being freed of limitations and again, is there a lengthy discourse or even a magic word that is the gatekeeper to that experience? Probably not. The language is symbolic. I believe that the language in the higher realms is also symbolic. As is music in this realm. And the quieter our minds are in our perceptions of those symbols, the more accurate our intuitions of their meanings are. Our projected desires or fears influence our perception of reality with symbols. A Rorschach test proves the point. The first time I ever saw one, there was one pattern that made me feel like I was seeing an explosion of possibilities. Standing back to look at this, you have to wonder, as we project onto others our desires asking, "What can you do for me?" and then interact with them to find out. What happens when you wash all your makeup off or lose your youth and vitality? When your number of choices and opportunities begins to decline with age? How then are we symbolized? I say this to indicate that it is in our nature to communicate in symbols and to impart meaning even to the simplest things.

We *want* things to be rich with information, a discovery unto themselves. We understand the spoken word has a certain amount of information but there is so much more to add when we consider body language, nuance, inflection, emotion, vocabulary and even the perfectly timed...pause.

Understanding the differences above provides the foundation upon which to see with non-linear understanding. It allows the worldly appreciation of life here, just like everyone else enjoys. It also allows seeing the intersection of probabilities before Choice collapses one of their waves into a moment of physical reality.

The will is free until it acts. The longer you can stand within that state of potential, the more power you build up your own. You've felt it; when you get two competing, but equally great, job offers or social engagements. The longer you put off deciding, the more the excitement builds for both, until you are about to pop with anticipation. To a point, the longer you wait to choose, the greater the anticipation on the part of the other parties as well. Knowing when to choose is an art developed through practice. It's like creating a vacuum and then aiming it with your intention. Nature will make all efforts to fill it (page 135: *Horror vacui"*, *"Nature abhors a vacuum"*; *Aristotle*).

Chapter Fifteen:

# Conclusion

This book is the story of the power of childhood dreams, being eternally curious and not taking "no" for an answer. It also demonstrates that when the student is ready, the teacher and the teaching experience will come. The spiritual path is not for the faint of heart. It can be a solitary one but doesn't have to be a lonely one.

I've shared my NDE, my understanding of it, and how my prior life before the experience seemed tailored to produce it as a natural and needed step in my personal evolution.

In the end, it's easier to find God than it is to become a Man.

Indeed, the man who fell from the sky is not the same who flew into it. And for walking some of my journey with me, neither are you. Thank you.

*Walking along the edge of a sand dune in the world's oldest desert, the Namib, Namibia, 1989. That's a wild Meerkat with me.*

# Acknowledgements

## 1. Family members

a.  Enid Bruton, my mother, with whom I sat in our yard swing growing up, talking about our shared hopes and dreams. Who showed me it was OK to dream big and do big.

b.  Dana Bruton, my wife and amazing mother to three beautiful children, who one day read my initial draft when I left it out. As my toughest critic, she pulls no punches and I was amazed and knew it was sincere when she said, "This is really good. This is what you should be doing". Thank you for encouraging me to the next step.

## 2. Lifesavers

a.  Greg Gubitosi, who had intended on a quiet afternoon of fishing but whose plans I drastically changed the day I crashed my plane in front of him. Greg, thank you for being there that day and for calling 911 and keeping me alive until the LifeStar helicopter could arrive and fly me out.

b.  The LIFE STAR medivac helicopter team and the staff at Hartford Hospital. What can I say? The most efficient and passionate team of medical professionals I have never met, because I was either in shock or in the In Between the duration of our time together. My life and the quality of my recovery says it all to which I add, "Well Done".

### 3. Editor

a. Beth Wareham, my editor, who patiently read my manuscript and with her patient guidance, brought me to the finish line of this first marathon. I look forward to future races and you are a great running buddy.

### 4. Agent & Publisher

a. Lisa Hagan, my agent and publisher, who had the vision and belief to give me a chance to share my story and the encouragement in driving all the way to North Carolina to meet me during one of my presentations for IANDS.

### 5. Coworker

a. Julia Bobkoff, my screenwriting partner and NDE friend, with whom much of our work time was spent talking and pondering the In Between. "If two or more are gathered in my Name…". Truer words were never spoken in regard to those who witness..

### 6. Advisers/sources of information

a. PMH Atwater, my informal guide and the single greatest source of NDE wisdom I know. It was her audiobook that spoke the loudest to me and literally guided me to her door. As a result, I have quoted her extensively in this book because I could not have said any of it better in my own words. Thank you, PMH.

b. Mary Helen Hensley, who, as a catalyst in my NDE journey, showed up at exactly the right moment to help me knit it all together. After listening to my presentation, Mary Helen and I sat for no less than seven hours and talked like old friends catching up. Then she introduced

me to Lisa and Beth, for which I'll always be grateful.
Tim Pitts, who has ceaselessly encouraged me to write
and speak about my life in every imaginable way.

## 7. Teachers

a.  Gurinder Singh Ji, the current spiritual head of Radha
    Soami Satsang Beas, whose initiation I waited for
    my entire life and without whom I would not have
    had the foundation needed to understand this most
    transformational experience and see more clearly the
    journey Home.

## 8. Inspirations

a.  People everywhere, those who were, who are and who
    will be, who live their lives dedicated to something larger
    than themselves and point the way Home for us all.

# Author Bio

Jim Bruton has lived a life many people dream of but few experience. As a little boy, he lived within an active imagination including a love for wildlife filming, international travel, science fiction and vintage aviation. In adulthood, he checked every one of those off his list with internationally recognized achievements, an Emmy for a National Geographic wildlife film, traveling to all seven continents, the Titanic, the North Pole and Mt. Everest, shrinking a satellite TV truck into a backpack and transmitting live video from places before impossible and building and flying historical reproduction aircraft from World War 1 and the early 1930s.

For many, any one of these adventures resulted in a single lifetime achievement. For Jim, it was just the beginning, climaxing with the crash of his last aircraft and the Near-Death Experience that followed.

For more information please contact
The International Association
for Near-Death Studies (IANDS)

www.IANDS.org

919-383-7940

INTERNATIONAL ASSOCIATION
FOR NEAR DEATH STUDIES, INC
services@iands.org   919-383-7940

EXPLORE THE EXTRAORDINARY